RADIO AND TELEVISION:

A Selected, Annotated Bibliography

Supplement One: 1977-1981

compiled by

William E. McCavitt

The Scarecrow Press, Inc.
Metuchen, N.J., & London
1982

Library of Congress Cataloging in Publication Data

McCavitt, William E., 1932-
    Radio and television.

    Includes index.
    1. Broadcasting--Bibliography. I. McCavitt,
William E., 1932-   . Radio and television.
II. Title: Radio and television : a selected,
annotated bibliography. Supplement one, 1977-1981.
Z7221.M23   Suppl. [PN1990.8] 016.38454   82-5743
ISBN 0-8108-1556-7   AACR2

TABLE OF CONTENTS

iii

PREFACE

The basic volume of this selected, annotated bibliography contained 1100 listings of books and other print materials associated with all aspects of broadcasting. The listings included materials spanning a time period from 1920 to 1976.

This supplement contains approximately half that number of listings and covers the five-year span from 1976 to late 1981. The information revolution has indeed descended upon the broadcast field.

Once again, the books and other material included in this reference were, for the most part, made available to me by publishers and other professional groups. Their continued cooperation is very much appreciated.

The facilities of the Stapleton Library at Indiana University of Pennsylvania, The Pattee Library at the Pennsylvania State University and the Library of Congress have been essential in pursuing this work.

A book such as this is not and cannot be the work of a single individual. Many people suggest, recommend and contribute leads to new books. To those who helped I extend my thanks (and keep those book lists coming in for the next supplement). A special thanks to my Research Assistant, Helen Clinton, who spent many long hours going through stacks of reference materials, typing cards, alphabetizing materials and helping in the literature search.

I hope this continuation of <u>Radio and Television</u> will help guide future broadcasters in their research.

W. E. M.

INTRODUCTION

The literature on radio and television is growing at an incredible rate of speed. It is a sign of our times and reflects the increase in the technology related to these two areas. The field of audio and video broadcasting, and now non-broadcasting, is expanding and becoming increasingly complex.

This supplement is a guide to the literature that has been written over a relatively short period of time, compared to the basic volume. It is a selection from the total literature available. The purpose of this work and that of the first one is two-fold: 1) to guide institutional and personal collectors in the purchase of broadcasting books, and 2) to suggest what is still needed by showing what exists now.

The limitation of this book is that it is only a guide to selected books and periodicals in the field. To compile a comprehensive reference, even for a five-year period, which contained all the books and periodicals dealing with the existing and developing technologies related to broadcasting would be virtually impossible.

This volume is subject divided and includes some topics not included in the first volume. As before, within the major categories are numerous sub-categories. But each listing of books is in alphabetical order by author's last name. The major sections are:

1. <u>Surveys</u>: Broad reviews of most aspects of broadcasting. This is probably the best starting point for a casual reader interested in broadcasting today or in the past.

2. <u>History</u>: Included here are only those general volumes which intend to tell radio and/or television history in broad terms.

3. <u>Regulation</u>: Includes government and self-regulation studies.

4. Organization: Volumes that deal with or stress advertising, management, and other business-oriented features of radio-TV are found here.

5. Programming: Includes general reviews and histories as well as the many volumes devoted to specific types of radio/TV content.

6. Production: Most how-to-do-it books are found here.

7. News: Includes such areas as writing, interviews, political news events, and broadcast news journalism.

8. Advertising: Advertising in both radio and television including theoretical and practical applications.

9. Minorities: A small but growing area with new volumes coming out more in recent years.

10. Responsibility: Volumes that deal with the responsibility of broadcasting in broad terms.

11. Society: Studies with a point of view. Emphasis on studies of broadcast impact and how to improve the system and its parts.

12. Criticism: Studies of a generally critical nature are included here.

13. Public Broadcasting: Includes histories, criticisms, reviews, and how-to-do-it studies for public and instructional television.

14. Audience: Descriptions, preferences, studies on the audience, and impact of broadcasting on the audience are found here.

15. Research: Research studies dealing with all aspects of broadcasting.

16. Broadcasting Careers: Includes career encouraging books.

17. International: Selective review of English-language works on other countries: system of broadcasting, international broadcasting, propaganda, and satellites.

18. Technical: Brief selection of technical and technical-related books.

19. Cable Television: Studies of both general and specific natures on this type of broadcasting are found in this section.

20. Corporate Video: A relatively new use of television, an example of the growth of video outside of the broadcast industry.

21. Home Video: Another example of non-broadcast ideo and the spread of home videotape recorders, video games, and video disc.

22. Videotext: The emerging technology of an informational delivery system utilizing video.

23. Satellites: Delivery system that has grown rapidly over the last decade and impacts on broadcast stations, cable systems, and individual home reception.

24. Bibliographies: Includes previously printed broadcasting bibliographies.

25. Annuals: Listing of annual publications relating to the broadcast field.

26. Periodicals: An alphabetical listing of broadcast periodicals.

27. References: Includes available broadcast references.

Each entry has a reference number, full indicia on author(s), title, city and place of publication, date of edition, and number of pages. The annotation is intended to describe briefly the book's contents and is not intended to serve as a critical analysis. Each entry closes by giving a listing of supplementary items (such as photographs, illustrations, bibliographies, or indexes) if they are included in the work.

Below most sub-headings is a listing of cross-reference numbers that also pertain to the topic. Essential bibliographic details are given in full for each entry. The Appendix lists references that are not annotated nor subject classified since copies of the books were not obtained. They were included since it was felt that they were of significance.

In this volume, once again, the compiler had to make certain judgments. Books that have been omitted were either not found during the literature search or were omitted deliberately.

As in any work of this nature, this book is already out of date by the time it is published. To keep up-to-date in this field today would mean reading an almost constant flow of material being published in this electronic era. Book reviews in professional journals is one way of keeping up with new literature. At least it gives one a flavor of what is being written. Perhaps, sometime in the future, we will undertake this task again and provide a second supplement of this reference.

1. SURVEYS

A. RADIO

See also nos. 37, 39, 40, 42, 52.

1 Fornatale, Peter, and Joshua E. Mills. Radio in the Television Age. Woodstock, N.Y.: Overlook Press, 1980. 212 pp.

   Covers the last 30 years of radio in a chronological fashion, with special chapters on radio news, FM and public radio. Various formats are discussed. A well balanced book on radio. Bibliography and index.

2 Hastings, John. Fundamentals of Radio Broadcasting. New York: McGraw-Hill, 1980. 205 pp.

   Covers practically every aspect of radio broadcasting in fourteen chapters, reviewing government regulation and licensing, station equipment, programming, promotion of financing of a station. Includes suggested activities at the end of each chapter. Glossary, bibliography, and index.

3 Hilliard, Robert L., editor. Radio Broadcasting. 2nd edition, revised and enlarged. New York: Hastings House, 1976. 312 pp.

   A basic text of the principles and techniques of modern radio broadcasting. It has now been expanded and revised to reflect the further growth of radio and the development of new programming formats. Index, bibliography, illustrations, and photographs.

4 Whetmore, Edward J. The Magic Medium: An Introduction to Radio in America. Belmont, Calif.: Wadsworth Publishers, 1981. 275 pp.

1

Traces the development of radio from its meager
beginnings to the giant entertainment networks of the
"golden years," and finally to today's use of the medium. Included is comprehensive coverage of such
topics as ratings and their interpretation, the business
of radio, radio production, the recording industries' impact, and employment in radio. Index.

B. TELEVISION

See also no. 52.

5 Cole, Barry, editor. Television Today: A Close-up
   View. New York: Oxford Press, 1981. 480 pp.

   Sixty-five articles from TV Guide that address the
   important questions people ask about contemporary television. Covering subjects that are as diverse as television itself, the articles range from discussion by
   Arnold Toynbee and Daniel Boorstin on Television and
   Society to David Brinkley's Criteria for Television Net-
   worthiness and Isaac Asimov's and Alvin Toffler's Pre-
   dictions for the Effect of Television on the Future. It
   reveals who watches television; what the ratings are--
   and if they are valid; the truth about TV news coverage
   --the main source of news for two-thirds of the popu-
   lation; who decides what programs appear; and to what
   extent TV sex and violence affect society. Index.

6 Friendly, Fred. Due to Circumstances Beyond Our Control. New York: Vintage, 1978. 339 pp.

   An important account of the television industry as
   well as an analysis of how it got that way.

7 Hilliard, Robert L., editor. Television Broadcasting:
   An Introduction. New York: Hastings House Publishers, 1978. 376 pp.

   Provides a comprehensive survey of the world of
   television. Eight prominent broadcast educators review
   the major areas of TV including organization and impact, producing, writing, directing, and cable and alternative systems. Illustrations, notes, bibliography,
   and index.

8 Schneider, Ira, and Beryl Korot, editors. Video Art:

An Anthology. New York: Harcourt Brace Jovanovich, 1976. 286 pp.

Provides comments on video installation, history,
applications, video's role as an instrument of change,
etc. The book is divided into several sections of
which by far the longest is the heavily-illustrated section on video art. Illustrations.

9 Stuart, Fredric. The Effects of Television on the Motion Picture and Radio Industries. New York: Arno
   Press, 1976.

   This work is one of the few thorough analyses of
   this important topic. The author demonstrates that
   the introduction of television was the principal factor
   in bringing about the decline of the motion picture industry in the mid-fifties. Illustrations.

C. GENERAL

See also nos. 52, 143, 299.

10 Bittner, John R. Broadcasting: An Introduction.
    Englewood Cliffs, N.J.: Prentice-Hall, Inc., 1980.
    508 pp.

    Explores every aspect of broadcasting, from the
    human components to new technology. The author ex-
    plores the connections between the audience and the
    effects of broadcasting in society. Besides radio,
    television, and cable, other areas are discussed briefly,
    such as television in industry, satellites, and syndi-
    cation. Bibliography, instructor's manual, illustra-
    tions, glossary, appendix, index, and photographs.

11 Bittner, John R. Mass Communications: An Introduc-
    tion. 2nd edition. Englewood Cliffs, N.J.: Prentice-
    Hall, Inc., 1980. 442 pp.

    This new edition introduces the readers to the ex-
    panding realm of the mass media: newspapers, maga-
    zines, radio, television, film, books, and records.
    All of these diverse media are compared and shown
    in relationship to one another. Also included are the
    new technologies of communication. Case studies,
    glossary, and illustrations.

12 Chester, Giraud; Garnet R. Garrison; and Edgar E. Wil-
    lis. Television and Radio. 5th edition. Englewood
    Cliffs, N. J.: Prentice-Hall, 1978. 543 pp. Instruc-
    tor's Manual.

    The text retains the same straightforward format
    and structure followed in the previous four editions.
    Part I deals with radio and television in society, with
    attention to its history, organization and socioeconomic
    impact. Part II deals with the studio concerning sta-
    tion operation and organization; technical aspects, skills
    and techniques in announcing, acting, and directing.
    Photographs, bibliography, illustrations, index, and
    glossary.

13 DeFleur, Melvin L. , and Everette E. Dennis. Under-
    standing Mass Media. Boston, Mass.: Houghton Miff-
    lin, 1980. 516 pp.

    Divided into four parts: the nature of mass com-
    munication; the communication industries; impact and
    consequences of mass communication; outgrowth and
    outlook of mass communication. Glossary, index, and
    instructor's manual.

14 Emery, Michael, and Ted Curtis Smythe. Readings in
    Mass Communications: Concepts and Issues in the
    Mass Media. 3rd edition. Dubuque, Iowa: Wm. C.
    Brown, 1977. 281 pp.

    This book contains many new pieces. It attempts
    to hold a balance between "conceptual" material and
    articles which describe the function of the particular
    medium of communication. The format for this vol-
    ume remains the same as the others, mainly "Changing
    Concepts of the Function and Role of the Mass Media,"
    "Revolution in the Mass Media" and "Multiplying Media
    Debates." Index and photographs.

15 Fedler, Fred. An Introduction to the Mass Media. New
    York: Harcourt Brace Jovanovich, Inc. , 1978. 425
    pp.

    This book covers all the topics commonly treated in
    media courses, devoting separate chapters to each of
    the media: newspapers, news agencies, radio and tele-
    vision, advertising and public relations, films, maga-
    zines and books. Illustrations, photographs, and bibli-
    ographies.

16 Fischer, Heinz-Dietrich, and Stefan Reinhard Melnik, editors. Entertainment: A Cross-Cultural Examination. New York: Hastings House Publishers, 1979. 330 pp.

This collection of twenty-six articles, written by leading mass communication experts from twelve countries, investigates various aspects of entertainment as communication. Attention is focused primarily upon entertainment as provided by its current most important source--Mass Media. Bibliography, illustrations, charts, tables, and index.

17 Foster, Eugene S. Understanding Broadcasting. Reading, Mass.: Addison-Wesley Publishing Company, 1978. 494 pp. Instructor's Manual.

This text seeks to enable students first to understand the history, development and current operations of broadcasting in order to understand the issues and controversies surrounding the field. This is one of the better organized books dealing with surveys of broadcasting that have been released within the past five years. Index, bibliography, glossary, appendix, photographs, and graphs.

18 Gross, Lynne S. See/Hear: An Introduction to Broadcasting. Dubuque, Iowa: Wm. C. Brown, 1979. 368 pp.

Still another book on the history of broadcasting. This one is well illustrated and gives an overview of the field of broadcasting. Controversial aspects of broadcasting are presented for student analysis. The book also looks at the present and future of broadcasting. An instructor's manual is also available for the text. Index, glossary, photographs, and charts.

19 Hiebert, Ray Eldon; Donald F. Ungurait; and Thomas W. Bohn. Mass Media: An Introduction to Modern Communication. 2nd edition. New York: Longman, Inc., 1978. 512 pp.

Surveys all the mass media. Completely revised. It establishes a theoretical basis and sets forth a new conceptional view of the media--the Hub Model of Mass Communication. The authors discuss the practical as-

pects of the media, which is both timely and youth
oriented. Line and halftone illustrations, tables, bibliography, index, and charts.

20 Hybels, Saundra, and Dana Ulloth. Broadcasting: An
    Introduction to Radio and Television. New York: D.
    Van Nostrand, 1978. 320 pp.

        Information on how the broadcast industry functions
    and how it interacts with related organizations, such as
    rating services, advertisers, government regulatory
    agencies, researchers, and citizens groups. Book is
    designed for introductory course in broadcasting and
    includes an instructor's manual. Index, photographs,
    and graphs.

21 McGillem, Clare D. , and William P. McLauchlan. Hermes
    Bound: The Policy and Technology of Telecommunica-
    tions. West Lafayette, Ind. : Purdue University Office
    of Publications, n. d. 304 pp.

        The first three chapters of this book give a general
    introduction to the technology, the politics, and the
    economics of the telecommunications industry. The
    remainder of the book presents a variety of case studies
    relating to the development of telecommunications serv-
    ices and technology. These studies show the substan-
    tial influence that political and economic constraints
    have on technological development. Examples come
    from radio, television data transmission, satellite
    communications, the telephone, and related areas.
    Finally, the book examines projections of future de-
    velopments and proposes ways for effectively controlling
    such developments in a more equitable manner. Illus-
    trations, appendix, notes, and index.

22 Merrill, John C. , and Ralph R. Lowenstein. Media,
    Messages, and Men: New Perspectives in Communi-
    cation. 2nd Edition. New York: Longman, Inc. ,
    1979. 272 pp.

        The authors do not attempt to survey the field, but
    rather probe certain problem areas and issues, group-
    ed within broad categories--the changing roles of the
    media, the communicator and his audience, and media
    concepts and ethics. Annotated bibliography and index.

23 Moss, Mitchell L. , editor. Telecommunications and Pro-

ductivity. Reading, Mass.: Addison-Wesley Publishing Company, Inc., 1981. 396 pp.

Essays and notes collected at the international conference sponsored by the Center for Science and Technology Policy, Graduate School of Public Administration, New York University, January 29-30, 1980, which included experts from industry, government, and academia concerned with the use of new telecommunications systems. Sections range from potential of telecommunications and office of the future to the home (teletex, videotex, and consumer information data base) and public uses of telecommunications systems (teleconferencing and cable). Index.

24 Pember, Don R. Mass Media in America. Chicago: Science Research Associates, 1981.

Completely revised and updated chapters include history of print media, history of broadcasting, advertising and public relations, research and theory, the mass media business, the media today and tomorrow. Bibliography, index, and photographs.

25 Rissover, Fredric, and David C. Birch. Mass Media and the Popular Arts. 2nd edition. New York: McGraw-Hill Book Company, 1977. 384 pp.

Contains information on everything from production to aesthetics, to the psychology, sociology, rhetoric, and economics of mass media and the popular arts. Index and bibliography.

26 Robb, Scott H. Television/Radio Age Communications Coursebook. New York: Communications Research Institute, 1979. 400 pp.

The Coursebook meets an urgent need of broadcast educators, particularly those who teach the introductory course. It provides a current overview of the state of broadcasting. The looseleaf format makes it especially attractive since it can be updated on a yearly basis. Illustrations, charts, graphs, photographs, glossary, and index.

27 Rodman, George. Mass Media Issues: Analysis and Debate. Chicago: Science Research Associates, 1981.

Covers areas such as pornography and censorship,
television ratings, television news, television entertainment, sex and violence, minorities, and women.
Index.

28   Schrank, Jeffrey. Understanding Mass Media. Skokie,
     Ill.: National Textbook Company, 1981. 296 pp.

Primarily a text for the public schools. Covers all
aspects of mass media in a way that helps the students
to recognize the influence of mass media on their lives.
Index, photographs, and illustrations.

29   Seidle, Ronald J. Air Time. Boston: Allyn and Bacon,
     Inc.; Holbrook Press, Inc., 1977. 296 pp.

This book is geared to introducing courses in com-
pact broadcasting programs, covering everything from
roles of studio personnel to current production techniques. Coverage includes history, production tools
and techniques, station management, programming,
regulations, plus affiliation and ownership. Bibliography, glossary, index, and illustrations.

30   Smith, F. Leslie. Perspectives on Radio & TV: An In-
     troduction to Broadcasting in the United States. New
     York: Harper & Row, 1979. 512 pp.

All major areas of radio and television are surveyed
including entertainment, programming, news, commercials, and production. Alternative systems are also
discussed such as closed circuit television, theater television, closed captioning, home video recorders, and
video games. This book is written in a style that is
easy to understand. There is also an instructor's
manual with this text. Still another of the many books
on the history of broadcasting that have arrived on the
scene during the last five years. Index, bibliographies,
and charts.

31   Sterling, Christopher H. Broadcast Trends: Aspen In-
     stitute Guide to Radio, Television and Cable Statistics.
     New York: Praeger Publishers, 1980. 256 pp.

This book is part of a continuing series of focused
data collections drawn from the Mass Media: Aspen
Institute Guide to Communication Industry Trends. It

includes updated information and an introduction that provides a more focused synthesis of broadcasting trends and issues.

32   Sterling, Christopher, and Timothy R. Haight.   The Mass Media: Aspen Guide to Communications Industries Trends.   Palo Alto, Calif.:   Aspen Institute Publications;   Praeger Publishers, 1978.   457 pp.

The editors have gathered and analyzed historical and descriptive statistical information on the American mass media for academic, industry, trade, and government sources.   The information is presented and discussed in a topical, cross-related format, with a focus on the interrelationship and the trends among the various industries.   The industries covered in this volume are books, newspapers, magazines, motion pictures, recordings (discs and tape), radio (AM & FM), television, and cable.   Annotations, sources, and references.

33   Sterling, Christopher, and John M. Kittross.   Stay Tuned: A Concise History of American Broadcasting.   Belmont, Calif.:   Wadsworth, 1978.   550 pp.

One of the many new texts released during the past few years dealing with the history of broadcasting.   It covers all aspects of American broadcasting.   Photographs, bibliographies, appendixes, and outlines.

34   Summers, Harrison B.; Robert E. Summers; and John H. Pennybacker.   Broadcasting and the Public.   2nd revised edition.   Belmont, Calif.:   Wadsworth Publishing Company, 1978.   467 pp.

Expanded version of first edition, it reflects the increased regulatory activity that has taken place in the past decade.   Included also are some of the major criticisms of the services provided by radio and television. Good survey text.   Activity exercises have been added to the chapters.   Illustrations, index, and photographs.

35   Telecommunications: Trends and Directions.   Washington, D. C.:   Electronic Industries Association, 1981.   111 pp.

Covers all areas of telecommunications, including satellite communications and cable television.   Charts, diagrams, and illustrations.

36 Whetmore, Edward Jay. Mediamerica: Form, Content,
    and Consequence of Mass Communication. Belmont,
    Calif. : Wadsworth, 1979. 332 pp. Instructor's Man-
    ual.

        An introductory mass media text designed to develop
    a critical perspective for students as media consumers.
    In this up-to-date text, the author discusses what is
    happening as well as what has happened during the his-
    tory of mass media. Index, graphics, and references.

2. HISTORY

A. RADIO

37 DeLong, Thomas A. The Mighty Music Box: The Golden Age of Musical Radio. Los Angeles: Amber Crest Books, 1980. 335 pp.

   History of radio and radio stars. Good reference. Index, photographs, and bibliography.

38 Fornatale, Peter, and Joshua E. Mills. Radio in the Television Age. Woodstock, N.Y.: The Overlook Press, 1980. 212 pp.

   Comprehensive history of the past three decades of radio. Of interest to radio listeners, students and the industry, this book covers it all: the impact of commercial television on radio advertising, programming, listenership; the effects of inventions such as transistors; the creation of new formats, including top 40, classical, and disco; profiles of radio pioneers; radio news, deregulation of the airway; non-commercial radio; and more. Index and bibliography.

39 Leinwoll, Stanley. From Spark to Satellite: A History of Radio Communication. New York: Charles Scribner's Sons, 1979. 242 pp.

   Takes the reader from the beginning of wireless communications through broadcasting and satellite communications. There is also a chapter on future communications systems using lasers. Good reference. Bibliography, index, photographs, figures, and references.

40 MacDonald, J. Fred. Don't Touch That Dial: Radio Programming in American Life, 1920-1960. Chicago: Nelson-Hall, 1979. 412 pp.

11

Divided into two sections, this book first traces the history of radio and its programs, then it looks closely at distinct types of programs or social themes within radio during this time span. The contents include dialogue from actual radio shows, broadcasting as radio comedy, detective shows, westerns, broadcast journalism, soap operas and blacks in radio. Good complete history. Index, bibliography, and photographs.

41 Pusateri, C. Joseph. Enterprise in Radio: WWL and the Business of Broadcasting in America. Washington, D. C.: University Press of America, 1980. 366 pp.

A business history of one of the nation's oldest and most influential broadcasting stations, WWL in New Orleans. While tracing the WWL story from the crystal set days of the 1920's, the station's experience is placed within the wider context of the developing broadcasting industry in the U. S. Index and bibliography.

42 Rosen, Philip T. The Modern Stentors: Radio Broadcasting and the Federal Government, 1920-1934. Westport, Conn.: Greenwood Press, 1980. 270 pp.

Covers such topics as the struggle within government for control of radio, the operations of the department of Commerce and Secretary Hoover, organization of the industry, interference problems, creation of the Federal Radio Commission, the rise of network radio, the struggle for noncommercial stations and an overview of what can be learned today from these developments. Bibliography and index.

43 Wertheim, Arthur Frank. Radio Comedy. New York: Oxford University Press, 1979. 384 pp.

Discussion of the many radio comedies of the 1930's and 1940's. Explores the relationship between social history and radio comedy. Photographs.

B. TELEVISION

44 Howard, Herbert, and S. L. Carroll. Subscription Television: History, Current Status and Economic Projections. Washington, D. C.: National Association of Broadcasters, 1980. 178 pp.

Deals with the development of STV, on-air stations and economics of STV operations.

45 Shanks, Bob. The Cool Fire. New York: Vintage Books, 1978. 336 pp.

Written by the programming vice-president of ABC, this is a behind-the-scene account of commercial television, filled with anecdotes and historical and technical materials, that tell anyone interested in a TV career everything they need to know about the industry and how to be successful in it. Charts.

C. BIOGRAPHIES AND AUTOBIOGRAPHIES

46 Dreher, Carl. Sarnoff: An American Success. New York: Quadrangle, 1977. 282 pp.

A reasonably objective biography of the late guiding hand of RCA by a former colleague. Recounts Sarnoff's achievements.

47 Klurfeld, Herman. Winchell: His Life and Times. New York: Praeger, 1976. 212 pp.

An informal biography of Walter Winchell. There is a good deal here on how the columnist worked his way into the lives of the people he reported about.

48 MacVane, John. On the Air in World War II. New York: William Morrow and Company, 1979. 384 pp.

A vivid personal account that is at once high adventure and authoritative, informative history. NBC's chief radio correspondent in the European theater tells about his assignments during World War II. Interesting look at WWII from a correspondent's point of view. Index and photographs.

49 Paley, William S. As It Happened. New York: Doubleday and Company, Inc., 1979. 418 pp.

Excellent book written by one of the people who helped develop broadcasting (CBS in particular) as we know it today. Good insight into the making of a major network. Interesting look at the people associated with Paley, also. Index, illustrations, appendix, and photographs.

50   Thomas, Lowell. Good Evening Everybody. New York:
     Avon Books. 1977. 333 pp.

          Paperback dealing with the history of news coverage
     by Lowell Thomas, written by Thomas. An interesting
     account of broadcast history written by one who lived it.
     A remarkable story. Photographs.

D.   GENERAL

See also nos. 12, 17, 18, 20, 29, 30, 33, 299.

51   Baker, John C. Farm Broadcasting: The First Sixty
     Years. Ames, Iowa: Iowa State University Press,
     1981. 342 pp.

          A history of farm broadcasting from its origins in
     1920 up to the present day, covering local, regional
     and national programs. The author shows how these
     daily broadcasters, dispensing information on weather,
     market prices, government actions, and technological
     developments have changed the course of farming and
     society in America.

52   Campbell, Robert. The Golden Years of Broadcasting: A
     Celebration of the First Fifty Years of Radio and TV
     on NBC. New York: Simon & Schuster, Inc. , 1976.
     256 pp.

          Good pictorial history of the broadcast industry. In-
     teresting reading for both the believer and the non-be-
     liever. Photographs.

53   Csida, Joseph, and June Bundy Csida. American Enter-
     tainment. New York: Watson-Guptill Publications
     (Billboard Books), 1978. 448 pp.

          Story of the interrelationships of all phases of Amer-
     ican show business. Divided into six chronological parts
     constituting a comprehensive history of popular show
     business. Photographs, illustrations, index, and bib-
     liography.

54   Desmond, Robert W. The Information Process: World
     News Reporting to the Twentieth Century. Iowa City,
     Iowa: University of Iowa Press, 1977. 445 pp.

This comprehensive survey of world news reporting
has a new focus and detailed presentation that makes it
a unique contribution to communications history. The
content ranges from the invention of the alphabet, paper
and ink, and the printing press to the perfection of the
mass communications system. Index and bibliography.

55 Desmond, Robert W. Windows on the World: World News
Reporting--1900-1920. Iowa City, Iowa: University of
Iowa Press, 1977. 608 pp.

In this volume, as in The Information Process above,
each significant development in the history of the press
is cogently related to the political, social, and economic events of the time. This book surveys newsmaking
and newsgathering within the frame of the scientific ad-
vances of the early 1900's, including radio. Index and
bibliography.

56 Gordon, George N. The Communications Revolution: A
History of Mass Media in the United States. New York:
Hastings House Publishers, 1977. 338 pp.

Includes the social, cultural, political, and economic
backgrounds of the colonial period to the present. Newspapers, movies, radio and television are traced from
their beginnings to the present day in a single narrative, with emphasis upon the way each medium has influenced the nation and each other in its development,
both as technology and as culture. Bibliography and
index.

57 Quinlin, Sterling. Inside ABC: American Broadcasting
Company's Rise to Power. New York: Hastings House,
1979. 290 pp.

Complete and candid history by a former ABC executive that offers a uniquely revealing look into the top
levels of the broadcast industry. Photographs, bibliography, and index.

58 Stevens, John D. , and Hazel Dickens Garcia. Communication History. Beverly Hills, Calif.: Sage Publications, Inc. , 1980. 164 pp.

Includes the impact of public opinion on mass media
and the development of distribution systems of both
print and non-print media. References and index.

59 Will, Thomas E. Telecommunications Structure and Man-
    agement in the Executive Branch of Government, 1900-
    1970. Boulder, Colo.: Westview Press, 1978. 214
    pp.

    Reviews the early executive branch involvement in
    radio telecommunications, the Radio Act of 1927 and the
    Communications Act of 1934, the technological advance
    of radio telecommunications and its effect on the execu-
    tive branch before and after World War II, the appoint-
    ments of telecommunications advisors to presidents from
    1951 to 1967, and the creation of the President's Task
    Force in 1967 to deal with the problems created by an
    inherently limited radio spectrum. Notes, appendix,
    and bibliography.

3. REGULATION

A. FCC

See also nos. 66, 67, 73, 74, 78, 80, 81, 82, 84, 87, 88, 89, 96, 97, 101, 192, 379, 380, 389, 393.

60 Cole, Barry, and M. Oettinger. Reluctant Regulators: The FCC and the Broadcast Audience. revised edition. Reading, Mass.: Addison-Wesley Publishing Company, 1978. 288 pp.

An inside look at the conflicts and compromises that temper the Federal Communications Commission's broadcasting decisions. Some of the more dramatic stories in this book involve confrontations between FCC regulators and groups and individuals who have no direct financial interest in broadcast. Appendix and index.

61 Emery, Walter B. Broadcasting and Government: Regulations and Responsibilities. revised and enlarged edition. East Lansing, Mich.: Michigan State University Press, n. d.

An important part of this volume is concerned with the broadcast spectrum, its character and utility for communications and the technical rules which govern the allocation of radio frequencies and their uses by various classes of stations as prescribed by the FCC. Still another section deals with the hard facts of regulation--governmental requirements that must be met to get a license, responsibilities that must be assumed, and conduct that must be avoided if one is to keep a license.

62 Jones, William K. Cases and Materials on Electronic Mass Media: Radio, Television and Cable. 2nd edition. New York: Foundation Press, 1979. 545 pp.

Updated version of the 1976 edition, this volume also focuses on the regulations of radio, television, and cable by the FCC in accordance with enabling federal legislation and subject to judicial review in the federal courts.   Appendix.

63   National Association of Broadcaster's Legal Guide to FCC Broadcast Rules, Regulations and Policies.   Washington, D. C.:   NAB, 1977.   600 pp.

Contents include deadlines, application and filing process, programming policies and practices, announcements, commercial policies, contests and promotions, ascertainment, equal opportunity employment, etc.   Reprints many FCC and NAB regulatory documents.   Index.

64   When Citizens Complain: UCC vs. FCC a Decade Later. New York: Communications Media Center, New York Law School, 1978.   32 pp.

Collection of papers tracing the legal, political, and economic dynamics of the citizen's group movement in broadcasting.

B.   PROGRAM CONTROL

See also no. 218.

65   Schmidt, Benno Jr.   Freedom of the Press vs. Public Access.   New York: Praeger Publishers, 1976.   312 pp.

Provides a general review of broadcast regulations and print-media problems relating to access.   Explores whether or not access obligations sustained for the electronic media are constitutionally barred for the print media.

C.   FAIRNESS

See also nos. 17, 33.

66   Friendly, Fred.   The Good Guys, the Bad Guys and the First Amendment: Free Speech vs. Fairness in Broadcasting.   New York: Vintage, 1978.   288 pp.

An examination of how the right to free speech is affected by government regulations attempting to insure fairness in broadcasting. Arguments both for and against the fairness doctrine are presented by documenting a series of legal battles it provided.

67 Simmons, Steven J. The Fairness Doctrine and the Media. Berkeley, Calif.: University of California Press, 1978. 303 pp.

Legal and historical analysis in the form of several reprinted articles of the author, tracing development and problems of the Doctrine, and suggesting some remedies to bring broadcast and print practices more in line.

D. COPYRIGHT

See also no. 389.

68 Gordon, David. Problems in Law of Mass Communications. Mineola, N. Y.: Foundation Press, Inc., 1978.

Programmed problems pamphlet to be used with Nelson & Teeters' Law of Mass Communications, 3rd edition.

69 Lawrence, John Shelton, and Bernard Timberg, editors. Fair Use and Free Inquiry: Copyright Law and the New Media. Norwood, N. J.: Ablex Publishing Corporation, 1980. 384 pp.

Traces the impact of copyright law upon scholarship dealing with the new media radio, television, film, popular music, and comics. Systematic and timely, this text goes beyond print-related controversies to address the problems of scholars working in the media. Bibliography and index.

70 Orlik, Peter B. Broadcast Copywriting. Boston, Mass.: Allyn and Bacon, Inc./Holbrook Press, 1978. 425 pp.

This comprehensive and fully illustrated text covers the entire spectrum of broadcast copywriting, from radio ID's and program promos to television commercials and PSAs. The book is spiced with the insights of over 40 industry writing and media experts. The

book is designed for courses in radio and TV broadcast copywriting. Illustrations, appendixes, and index.

E. GENERAL

See also nos. 59, 96, 209, 300, 381, 382, 422, 425, 427.

71   Botein, Michael, and Scott Robb, editors.   Competition
     vs. Regulations: The Case of the Mass Media.   N. Y. :
     New York Law School, 1978.   213 pp.

        This collection of materials traces recent administra-
     tive and judicial developments in the law of the elec-
     tronic media.   It includes analysis and materials on
     topics such as the FTC's proposed ban on children's
     advertising.   Index.

72   Communications Law, 1980.   Two volumes.   New York:
     Practicing Law Institute, 1980.

        Volume I includes such topics as defending the news
     media in libel situations and access to trials.   Volume
     II includes such topics as pay cable TV, TV in the
     courtroom, and reporters' rights.

73   Francois, William E.   Mass Media Law and Regulation.
     2nd edition.   Columbus, Ohio: Grid Inc. , 1978.   616
     pp.

        Includes extensive coverage of libel laws with de-
     tailed coverage of emerging standards of care being
     adopted by various states concerning libel suits brought
     by private individuals.   Covers new developments in
     radio-tv regulations, plus many other topics.   Index,
     glossary, appendix, and tables.

74   Franklin, Marc A.   Cases and Materials on Mass Media
     Law.   Mineola, N. Y. :   Foundation Press, 1978.   878
     pp.

        Casebook intended to acquaint students with major
     aspects of media law and to provide an extended look
     at the tensions between legal regulation and the First
     Amendment.   Contents include "The Development of the
     Concept of Freedom of Expression"; "Business Aspects
     of Mass Media Enterprises"; "Legal Problems of Ga-

thering Information"; Restrictions on Content of Communication"; "Distribution Problems of Non-Broadcasting Media"; "Introduction to Broadcasting"; "Broadcast Licensing"; "Legal Control of Programming--Sources and Content. " Index and appendix.

75 Franklin, Marc A. 1978 Update Memorandum of Recent Developments. Mineola, N. Y. : The Foundation Press, Inc. , 1978.

For use with The First Amendment and the Fourth Estate: Communications Law for Undergraduates.

76 Franklin, Marc A. The First Amendment and the Fourth Estate: Communications Law for the Undergraduates. Mineola, N. Y. : Foundation Press, 1977. 727 pp.

The purpose of this book is to clarify the major legal doctrines that affect mass media. It is not necessary to be a lawyer to understand the cases in the field. After each principal case, or article, notes and questions explain unusual points, highlights, particularly significant parts, and suggests possible consequences. Index and appendixes.

77 Gillmor, Donald, and Jerome Barron. Mass Communications Law. 3rd edition. St. Paul, Minn. : West Publishing Company, 1979. 997 pp.

The contents in this casebook include the impact of the First Amendment in terms of theory, practice, and problems; libel and the journalist; privacy and the press; the journalist's privilege; the law of newsgathering; free press and fair trial; pornography; and regulation of radio and tv.

78 Ginsburg, Douglas H. Regulation of Broadcasting: Law and Policy Towards Radio, Television and Cable Communications. St. Paul, Minn. : West Publishing Company, 1979. 741 pp.

A legal casebook on broadcasting and cable with material on basics of regulation, control of entry, ownership issues, press freedom and license, the Fairness Doctrine, children's television, public broadcasting, etc. Appendixes.

79   Haight, Timothy R. , editor. Telecommunications Policy
      and the Citizen. New York: Praeger Company, 1979.
      296 pp.

      This book explores the impact of the proposed Re-
      write of the Communications Act on the average citizen
      and consumer.   It gives the critics of many of the cur-
      rent communications industries' practices in light of
      new issues and technologies.   Index.

80   Kahn, Frank. Documents of American Broadcasting.   3rd
      edition. New Jersey: Prentice-Hall, Inc. , 1978.   638
      pp.

      The third edition presents a comprehensive and con-
      venient collection of primary source materials central
      to an understanding of the recurring issues of broad-
      casting in the United States.   The author lays the foun-
      dation for a critical analysis of public policy and in-
      vites both beginning and advanced students to synthe-
      size their own views of key developments in the history
      of regulation of the field.   Index, glossary of legal ter-
      minology, and bibliography.

81   Krasnow, Erwin G. , and Lawrence D. Longley.   The
      Politics of Broadcast Regulation.   2nd edition.   New
      York: St. Martin's Press, 1978.   213 pp.

      The second edition contains expanded discussions of
      the roles of all of the major participants in the broad-
      cast decision-making process and reflects changes in
      each participant's strategy and effectiveness.   For ex-
      ample, there is a section detailing how Congress af-
      fected the making of broadcast policy from 1970 to
      1977.   The chapters on comparative license renewal
      challenges and describes the events occurring after the
      landmark Citizens' Communications Center decision.
      A new case study has been added on the growth of citi-
      zen's band radio in the mid-1970's.   Bibliography, in-
      dex, and illustrations.

82   Levin, Harvey J.   Fact and Fancy in Television Regula-
      tion: An Economic Study of Policy Alternatives.   New
      York: Russell Sage Foundation, 1980.   505 pp.

      The most ambitious and comprehensive study of tele-
      vision economics and regulations outside of the Federal

Government's efforts. The book, however, is not for the general reader in television economics and regulation. The book closely resembles a series of scholarly articles on separate, but related, television policy issues. Appendixes, index, and tables.

83 Litman, Barry Russell. The Vertical Structure of the Television Broadcasting Industry: The Coalescence of Power. East Lansing, Mich.: Michigan State University, 1979. 172 pp.

This is an adaptation of the author's dissertation. The work is defined as being an extension of the FCC's findings as reflected in its prime-time access rules, which were formulated when it became alarmed at the increasing trend toward vertical integration by contract and the allegations by program producers that without surrendering subsidiary rights and profit participations, they were denied access to network prime time. Chapters include: theories of vertical integration, the institutions of the broadcast industry, vertical integration by contract, the affiliation agreement, etc. Illustrations and bibliography.

84 Mosco, Vincent. Broadcasting in the United States. Norwood, N. J.: Ablex Publishing Corporation, 1979. 168 pp.

The author contends that the owners of radio and television situations have induced the FCC to act conservatively to FM radio, UHF TV, cable TV, and subscription TV. He believes also that this has resulted in the concentration of political and economic power in the hands of the broadcasting industry and has restricted the audiences' choice of programs. He reviews proposals that have been made to change the regulatory structure. Appendixes, bibliography, and index.

85 Nelson, Harold L., and Dwight L. Teeter, Jr. Law of Mass Communication. 3rd edition. Mineola, N.Y.: Foundation Press, Inc., 1978. 675 pp.

Revised and updated version of this widely adopted coursebook on mass media law. This third edition reflects the significant changes which have occurred during the last five years. It also reflects the landmark cases decided by the U. S. Supreme Court during recent terms. This edition comes with an instructor's manual. Tables of cases and index.

86 Owens, Bruce M. , and Ronald Braeutigam. The Regulation Game. Cambridge, Mass.: Ballinger Publishing Company, 1978. 271 pp.

As the title suggests, the book deals with regulations affecting many areas. One chapter is devoted to regulation of the new technology: cable television. Index, bibliography, and tables.

87 Pember, Don R. Mass Media Law. 2nd edition. Dubuque, Iowa: Wm. C. Brown, 1981. 513 pp.

The primary focus of this edition remains the same and that is the presentation of the law needed by a working journalist, broadcasters, or persons in advertising or public relations. Material in every chapter has been updated and a chapter on Regulation of the Press has been added. Good text for mass media law courses. Index, bibliographies, articles, tables of cases.

88 Rice, David M.; Michael Botein; and Edward B. Samuels. Development and Regulation of New Communications Technologies. New York: Communications Media Center, New York Law School, 1980. 140 pp.

This book examines the economic, legal and regulatory issues raised by the development of four new communications technologies--cable, STV, MDS, and DBS. The book begins by examining the economic basis for each service and discusses the applications in which they overlap and compete. (STV - Subscription; MDS - Multipoint Distribution Service; DBS - Direct Broadcast Satellites). Index.

89 Zuckman, Harvey, and Martin J. Gaynes. Mass Communications Law in a Nutshell. St. Paul, Minn.: West Publishing Company, 1977. 431 pp.

Intended as a basic text for communications law students. Part I deals with the First Amendment and mass communications. Part II deals with regulation and the media. Index.

4. ORGANIZATION

A. RADIO ECONOMICS

See also nos. 109, 111.

90 Hoffer, Jay, and John McRae. The Complete Broadcast Sales Guide for Stations, Reps and Ad Agencies. Blue Ridge Summit, Pa.: TAB Books, 1981. 252 pp.

Provides directed career guidance as well as specific pointers on day-to-day sales operations, mainly at the small AM and FM stations. TV is not included.

B. TELEVISION MANAGEMENT

See also nos. 57, 134, 135, 254, 299.

91 Davis, Douglas, and Allison Simmons, editors. The New Television: A Public/Private Art. Cambridge, Mass.: The MIT Press, 1976. 256 pp.

This book is based on an international conference of television of the future. It contains critiques, comments, and video art by various contributors. Illustrations.

92 DeLuca, Stuart M. Television's Transformation: The Next 25 Years. San Diego, Calif.: A. S. Barnes, 1980. 287 pp.

Shows how we came to have the present television industry and identifies the changes that are taking place right now, which are propelling television into a new era. It begins with the origin of today's television system, describing how the commercial networks of the 1930's and 1940's guided the emergence of television.

25

The new areas examined, such as cable TV, broadcast satellites, video recorders, discs, projectors and
teletext are covered as well. Good book for students
of mass communications and for those in the television
industry. Index and photographs.

93 Dessart, George, editor. Television in the Real World:
    A Case Study Course in Broadcast Management. New
    York: Hastings House, 1978. 448 pp.

    Based on a simulation of the process of filing a li-
    cense application for the new VHF TV station in a
    mythical American City. The book traces in detail
    the proceedings, procedures and problems involved in
    establishing a station. This book was written as a re-
    sult of the Fifth Annual IRTS Faculty/Industry Seminar.
    Charts, graphs, appendixes, and index.

C. NETWORKS

See also nos. 57, 246.

94 Bergreen, Lawrence. Look Now, Pay Later: The Role
    of Network Broadcasting. New York: Doubleday and
    Company, 1980. 300 pp.

    The author traces the 50-year rise of broadcasting.
    It is rich with information about the technology, the
    people, and the development of broadcasting. Bibliog-
    raphy and index.

95 Botein, Michael, and David Rise, editors. Network Tele-
    vision and the Public Interest. Lexington, Mass.: Lex-
    ington Books, 1980. 223 pp.

    The results of a conference held at the New York
    Law School on Network Television and the Public In-
    terest. Five principal speakers and sixteen panelists
    discussed the legal, economical and operational aspects
    of network television. The conference was held on Oc-
    tober 19-20 just as the FCC issued a new and expanded
    document in its Network Inquiry. Index and tables.

96 The Foreseeable Future of Television Networks: Legal
    Resource Manual. New York: New York Law School,
    1979. 408 pp.

Published in conjunction with UCLA's Communications Law Program, this book includes materials on the background, development, and current regulatory status of television networks. It includes edited versions of the leading Supreme Court and Court of Appeals cases, which defined the FCC's power in this field. Covered, also, are discussions of antitrust issues and new technologies. Charts.

97 Reel, A. Frank. The Networks: How They Stole the Show. New York: Scribner's Sons, 1979. 208 pp.

This book shows how the major networks, by serving their own private interests, have literally robbed television of its potential. This study goes back to the beginning of TV to explain how the FCC created the technical conditions for the network's monopoly of the air, how the network's acquired television stations in the nation's largest markets and how they gradually took over their affiliate's air time. Index.

D. GENERAL

See also nos. 20, 29.

98 Coleman, Howard W. Case Studies in Broadcast Management. 2nd edition. Revised and enlarged. New York: Hastings House Publishers, 1978, 160 pp.

Revised throughout and aimed to supplement Quaal and Brown's Broadcast Management. This book uses fictional accounts of real situations to encourage thinking and discussion about problems of operating radio and television stations.

99 Compaine, Benjamin M. , editor. Who Owns the Media? Concentration of Ownership in the Mass Communications Industry. White Plains, N. Y. : Knowledge Industry Publications, 1979. 368 pp.

Analyzes the ownership structure of each of the major mass media: daily newspapers, television, radio, magazines, books, films, cable, and pay TV. This study identifies the dominant owners in each medium, the extent of concentration, the effect of these ownership patterns on content and dissemination

of information and the degree of government control
and activity in each medium.   A well researched
book.   Index, bibliography, and tables.

100   Johnson, Joseph S. , and Kenneth K. Jones.   Modern
Radio Station Practices.   2nd edition.   Belmont,
Calif. :   Wadsworth Publishing Company, 1978.   418
pp.

An updated and reorganized edition including material on production.   It focuses on the principles
of radio in its entirety and then applies them by close
examination with 15 of the nation's most successful
stations.   It analyzes how programs get on the air,
what stations are trying to accomplish, and what appeals and strategies are used.   Appendixes, glossary,
diagrams, charts, photographs, and index.

101   "Purchasing a Broadcast Station: A Buyer's Guide. "
Washington, D. C. :   National Association of Broadcasters, 1978.   45 pp.

Discusses such things as searching for a station,
evaluating its worth and agreeing on price, financing
the purchase, the contract, and the role of the FCC.
Appendixes.

5. PROGRAMMING

A. NEWS/POLITICAL

See also nos. 50, 54, 55, 118, 189, 192, 206, 227, 282.

102 Adams, William, and Fay Schreibman, editors. Television Network News. Washington, D. C.: George Washington University, School of Public and International Affairs, 1978. 231 pp.

Discussions of some of the more important issues in the study of network news content. The three areas emphasized are the status of existing research; methodological issues; and future directions of research.

103 Barrett, Marvin. Rich News, Poor News: The Alfred I. DuPont Columbia University Survey of Broadcast Journalism. New York: Crowell, 1978. 344 pp.

Published every two years, this series dates back to 1968. It is a valuable analysis of the medium's strong and weak points on the national and local levels. Concentrating as before on television journalism, chapters review general trends and specific issues of the year. Index.

104 Bitzer, Lloyd, and Theodore Rueter. Carter vs. Ford: The Counterfeit Debates of 1976. Madison, Wisc.: University of Wisconsin Press, 1980. 428 pp.

Should be of interest to students of rhetoric. The authors provide an accurate transcript of the debates along with a detailed internal analysis of debate content.

105 Epstein, Edward Jay. Between Fact and Fiction. New York: Vintage Books, 1978. 320 pp.

29

An examination of the reporting of major recent
political events--the discovery of Watergate, the investigation into John F. Kennedy's assassination and
the Vietnam War to mention a few.

106 Epstein, Edward J. News from Nowhere: Television
     and the News. New York: Vintage Books, 1978.
     321 pp.

     A detailed examination of the evening's news pro-
     grams of ABC, CBS, and NBC which suggests that in-
     ternal corporate policy, rather than external circum-
     stances or long range goals, shape the direction of
     TV news coverage. Notes, bibliography, index.

107 Fang, Irving. Television News, Radio News. 3rd edi-
     tion. St. Paul, Minn.: Rada Press, 1980. 399 pp.

     Updated version of author's earlier Television News
     is a how-to guide for the broadcast student. Written
     in textbook style, it includes study questions at the
     end of each chapter and an instructor's manual.

108 Gans, Herbert J. Deciding What's News: A Study of
     CBS Evening News, NBC Nightly News and Time.
     New York: Pantheon, 1979. 393 pp.

     The fact is that the network newscasters and 99
     percent of journalists who are not celebrities are the
     prime regular suppliers of information about America
     for most Americans. That fact is the subject of this
     book. Part I describes how America is reported in
     the popular national news media; Part II indicates why
     it is so reported; and Part III proposes some other
     ways of reporting it. Index, bibliography, and tables.

109 Gates, Gary Paul. Air Time: The Inside Story of CBS
     News. New York: Harper and Row, 1978. 428 pp.

     This is a review of the post World War II develop-
     ment of the main on-air and behind-the-scenes per-
     sonnel at CBS radio and television news. Most of
     the book deals with the past 15 years of television
     journalism. Index.

110 Graber, Doris A. Crime News and The Public. New
     York: Praeger Publishers, 1980. 256 pp.

This book examines the nature of street and white collar crime news as reported in the mass media in three types of cities, and assesses its impact on the perceptions and actions of audiences. General and crime news content of five newspapers and five television channels was analyzed extensively during a one-year period. The author's findings show that the public's images of criminals and their mode of operation differ substantially from the images presented by the media.

111   Kierstead, Phillip O.   All News Radio.   Blue Ridge Summit, Pa.:   TAB Books, 1980.   225 pp.

Overview of the specialty radio format. Includes such things as staff, selling such programs to advertising, careers, and the technical aspects.

112   Kraus, Sidney, editor.   The Great Debates: Carter versus Ford.   Bloomington, Ind.:   Indiana University Press, 1979.   553 pp.

This book will be a useful reference for those interested in future study of presidential debates. Part I sets forth the background and perspective for the debates. Part II is devoted to empirical studies of the effects of the debates. The book should be a welcome addition to the literature of contemporary political studies.

113   Mitchell, Lee M.   With the Nation Watching.   Lexington, Mass.:   Lexington Books, 1979.   120 pp.

Televised presidential debates by the leading contenders for the nation's highest office should be a "regular and customary feature" of presidential campaigns. This task force report urges immediate action on the organization, financing, and format of the debates and suggests policy procedures in each area. Notes and references.

114   Patterson, Thomas E.   The Mass Media Election: How Americans Choose Their President.   New York: Praeger Publishers, 1980.   220 pp.

The main purpose of this book is to provide a body of knowledge that will contribute to the understanding

of the election coverage and the American voter.
Looking closely at the mass media election of today,
it studies ways in which voters respond to it, how
much attention they give it, what they learn from it,
how they are influenced by it, as well as press coverage of elections.   Index.

115   Powers, Ron.   The News-Casters: The News Business
      As Show Business.   New York: St. Martin's Press,
      1978.   243 pp.

      Contains revealing interviews with a number of the
      industry's leading journalists and mass communica-
      tions specialists.   It documents the encroachment of
      show biz into newscasting.   It also examines the prog-
      ress of television journalism.   Index.

116   Weaver, David H.; Doris A. Graber; Maxwell E. Mc-
      Combs; and Chaim H. Eyal.   Media Agenda--Setting
      in a Presidential Election.   New York: Praeger Pub-
      lishers, 1978.   457 pp.

      More than 1100 interviews with voters in three
      distinctly different communities and content analysis
      of thousands of newspaper and television stories are
      combined to produce the most thorough and definitive
      conclusions to date on the agenda setting effects of
      the media in a U.S. presidential campaign.   The con-
      cept of media agenda setting is explained to include
      candidates' images and political interests as well as
      issues during the entire presidential election year of
      1976.

117   Wolverton, Mike.   And Now the News.   Houston, Texas:
      Gulf Publishing Company, 1977.   136 pp.

      State of the art examination of the "new journa-
      lism."   It explores the tools and techniques necessary
      to the rapidly developing field of electronic journalism.
      The book includes broadcast style, editing and narra-
      tive techniques, camera presence, and determing what
      really is news.   Index and bibliography.

118   Yorke, Ivor.   The Technique of Television News.   New
      York: Focal Press (Hastings House), 1978.   240 pp.

      A realistic British approach to the problems of

putting TV news on the air. Topics it examines in
detail include the difference between written and spo-
ken journalism, how to match words to film, build
up a news item, carry out a reporting assignment,
and integrate the many different activities that make
up a TV news program. Illustrations.

B. PUBLIC AFFAIRS

119 Kierstead, Phillip. Modern Public Affairs Programming.
Blue Ridge Summit, Pa.: TAB Books, 1979. 251
pp.

This is an up-to-date guide to community public
affairs programming. It is written for broadcasting
executives and programmers. There is information
presented for both radio and television, explaining
methods of preparing and executing documentaries,
interviews, even quiz shows, along with practical examples of each type. Index, illustrations, and photographs.

120 Whedon, Peggy. Always on Sunday: 1000 Sundays with
Issues and Answers. New York: Norton, 1980. 272
pp.

The producers of the show talk about many of the
show's guests and about the show itself. The book is
more of a collection of memoirs than a hard study
of the news interview format.

C. DOCUMENTARIES

121 Hammond, Charles Montgomery, Jr. The Image Decade:
Television Documentary: 1965-1975. New York:
Hastings House Publishers, 1981. 285 pp.

This book describes the evolution of commercial
network television news and theme documentary during
the years of 1965 to 1975, offering theory, criticism,
history and practical illustrations. Provocative analysis of the work of outstanding documentary procedures
and reporters at NBC, CBS, and ABC are provided.
Bibliography and index.

D. DRAMA

122   Gianakos, Larry James. Television Drama Series Pro-
      gramming: A Comprehensive Chronicle, 1947-1959.
      Metuchen, N. J. : Scarecrow Press, 1980. 565 pp.

         The book begins with a short overview chapter of
      detailed "days and times" showing TV schedules, then
      lists the shows. Credits are given for the regulars
      in each series plus for the guest stars in all episodes.

123   Greenburg, Bradley S. Life on Television: Content
      Analysis of U. S. TV Drama. Norwood, N. J. : Ab-
      lex Publishing Corporation, 1980. 224 pp.

         Represents the first scholarly attempt to identify,
      document, and analyze the major dimensions--social,
      sexual, and racial--of U. S. prime time TV content.
      By examining fictional TV series run in prime-time
      and on Saturday mornings over three seasons, the
      author and his research team have put together a
      fascinating study of American society according to
      TV. References, index, and tables.

124   LeMay, Harding. Eight Years in Another World. New
      York: Atheneum Publishers, 1981. 246 pp.

         A behind-the-scenes look at the world of soap
      operas. Written by an award winning writer of one
      of television's most popular day time serials, "An-
      other World". The author tells of power struggles
      with producers, directors, stars and advertising ex-
      ecutives. He talks about the special problems of wri-
      ting for a form that has no beginning or end but "is
      one endless middle. "

125   Stedman, Raymond William. The Serials: Suspense and
      Drama by Installment, 2nd edition. Norman: Univer-
      sity of Oklahoma Press, 1977. 574 pp.

         Since its first publication in 1971, The Serials has
      been a standard history of that indestructible drama
      form, the serial. This new edition, revised and en-
      larged, includes new programs, such as the latest
      productions of Masterpiece Theatre; Rich Man Poor
      Man; the Waltons; Mary Hartman, Mary Hartman; and
      the newcomers to the daytime soaps. Index, bibliog-
      raphy, and photographs.

E. VARIETY

126 Metz, Robert. The Tonight Show. New York: Playboy
     Press, 1980. 290 pp.

        This story of the Carson show is based on research
     and interviews. The book is a full history of the show,
     including the Paar period. It is not altogether flatter-
     ing to the king of the evening hour.

F. CHILDREN

See also nos. 139, 209, 210, 211, 240, 249, 250, 280, 285,
297, 314, 315.

127 Barcus, F. Earle, and Rachel Wolkin. Children's Tele-
     vision: An Analysis of Programming and Advertising.
     New York: Praeger Publishers, 1977. 252 pp.

        Discusses the increasing interest in issues affecting
     children's television since 1960. Analyzes the re-
     search findings of more than 55 hours of monitored
     weekend and after school children's programming and
     advertising. Covers the structure, content, populari-
     ty, characters, advertising, racial and sexual stereo-
     typing and violence in both programming and adver-
     tising. Appendix and tables.

128 Harmonay, Maureen, editor. Promise and Performance:
     Children with Special Needs. ACT's Guide to TV
     Programming for Children, Volume 1. Cambridge,
     Mass.: Ballinger, 1977. 255 pp.

        This book includes discussions of some of the ways
     in which children who are disabled perceive them-
     selves; how presumably normal children develop per-
     ceptions of others with handicaps; and the interactions
     between the two. There is also a treatment of the
     role that the family and adults can play in helping
     children with special needs. Index, bibliography,
     photographs, illustrations, and tables.

129 Harmonay, Maureen, editor. Promise and Performance:
     The Arts. ACT's Guide to TV Programming for Chil-
     dren, Volume 2. Cambridge, Mass.: Ballinger, 1979.
     216 pp.

Book includes discussions of the arts and television programming for children. This volume, as was the first, was initiated by the Action for Children's Television organization. Articles included have been written by people from various areas including the arts, industry, educators, and media management. Index, figures, and photographs.

130   Kaye, Evelyn. The A. C. T. Guide to Children's Television: How to Treat TV with TLC. Revised edition. Boston, Mass.: Beacon Press, 1979. 226 pp.

Basic resource handbook for parents and concerned citizens from Action for Children's Television, a nationwide group advocating quality television. It offers invaluable advice on how to make TV a positive force in a child's life. Appendix, bibliography, illustrations, photographs, and figures.

131   Palmer, Edward L. , and Aimee Dorr, editors. Children and the Faces of Television: Teaching, Violence, Selling. New York: Academic Press, 1980. 360 pp.

The authors span the disciplines of psychology, education, sociology, law and communication. Areas covered include history of educational broadcasting, television for instruction, the impact of television violence, effects of television advertising on children and much more. An outstanding collection of reviews and commentaries.

132   Turow, Joseph. Entertainment, Education, and the Hard Sell. New York: Praeger Publishers, 1981. 160 pp.

An analysis of commercial children's television. This book examines the diversity of programming and stages in the evolution of contemporary children's television during the decades of the fifties, sixties, and seventies.

G.   GENERAL

See also nos. 40, 51, 97, 213, 246, 277, 278, 281, 284, 307, 308, 311.

133   Andrews, Bart, and Brad Dunning. The Worst TV Shows
      Ever. New York: Dutton, 1980. 203 pp.

         The author has chosen 30 of 3500 programs as the
      worst. He explains why, with brief plot synopsis,
      contemporary reviews, and full credits.

134   Bedell, Sally. Up the Tube: Prime-Time TV and the
      Silverman Years. New York: The Viking Press,
      Inc., 1981. 313 pp.

         The story of how prime-time programming devel-
      oped during the seventies. The author follows the
      career of Fred Silverman as he makes his way through
      all three major networks. Up the Tube probes the
      Silverman legend, the myths and stories surrounding
      his successes and failures, and separates what he did
      do from what he didn't do to prime-time TV.

135   Cantor, Muriel G. Prime-Time Television: Content and
      Control. Beverly Hills, Calif.: Sage Publications,
      1980. 144 pp.

         Seven chapters containing background information
      on TV drama, methodology, history and content analy-
      sis. The major focus is an examination of the way
      different groups and corporations interact in their ef-
      forts to gain control over one another and subsequent-
      ly over the content of prime-time TV drama.

136   Clift, Charles III, and Archie Greer, editors. Broadcast
      Programming: The Current Perspective. 6th edi-
      tion. Washington, D.C.: University Press of Ameri-
      ca, 1980. 243 pp.

         College level text for radio and TV broadcasting
      courses. The collection of readings includes reprinted
      articles and reference material on ratings and pro-
      gramming for both radio and TV. Detailed analysis
      of prime-time programming from 1973 to 1979. This
      sixth edition has many new features including revised
      TV ratings book, added sections on radio formats,
      new sections on network TV programming, etc. Sam-
      ple FCC forms and figures.

137   Eastman, Susan Tyler; Sydney W. Head; and Lewis Klein.
      Broadcast Programming: Strategies for Winning Tele-

vision and Radio Audiences.   Belmont, Calif. :   Wadsworth Publishing Company, 1981.   350 pp.

This text deals with decision making in programming from a day-to-day managerial point of view
through chapters by professionals in the field.   Describes and analyzes the differences among types of
stations, types of programming and emerging services
such as pay TV.   Glossary, bibliography, and index.

138   Hall, Claude, and Barbara Hall.   This Business of Radio
       Programming.   Cincinnati, Ohio: Billboard Books,
       1977.   360 pp.

The first part of the book explores the background
of programming: research, promotion, production,
engineering, broadcasting schools, salaries and the
controversial topic of Payola.   The second part is a
collection of interviews with key people in radio who
speak openly about the realities of the business.
Glossary, index, and bibliography.

139   Lesser, Gerald S.   Children and Television: Lessons
       from "Sesame Street."   New York: Vintage Books,
       1978.   240 pp.

Tells the story of the people who created Sesame
Street, the ideas that went into it, and the insights
about children that emerged from it.   Illustrations,
references, and index.

140   Reiss, David S.   M*A*S*H: The Exclusive, Inside Story
       of TV's Most Popular Show.   Indianapolis, Ind. :
       Bobbs-Merrill, 1980.   159 pp.

Primarily a fan's book, the information on writers
and producers and the plots of all episodes, make
this book a reference source.

141   Routt, Edd; James B. McGrath; and Fredric Weiss.   The
       Radio Format Conundrum.   New York: Hastings
       House, 1978.   314 pp.

This book explores the many basic commercial radio formats in use in the United States today, along
with some of the known variations.   The descriptions
of the formats include, not only the basic character-

istics and the advantages and disadvantages of each, but also covers the mechanics of constructing such formats. Photographs, bibliography, index, glossary, illustrations, and charts.

142 Smith, V. Jackson. Programming for Radio and Television. Washington, D. C.: University Press of America, 1980. 136 pp.

Covers programming past and present. Identifies audiences plus listening and viewing habits. Characteristics of good programs and program evaluations are discussed. Charts and glossary.

6. PRODUCTION

A. AUDIO

143 Alten, Stanley R. <u>Audio in Media.</u> Belmont, Calif.:
Wadsworth Publishing Company, 1981. 428 pp.

The book was written to help close the gap between
the importance of audio in media and its lack of re-
cognition. It was written to treat the subject of audio
generally by providing a broad theoretical and practical foundation in the techniques and aesthetics of
sound and by applying them to the particular demands
of radio, television, film, and music productions. Finally, it was written to introduce audio using a non-
technical approach and to avoid reference to makes
and models of equipment, prescribed techniques and
rules. All objectives were met. Index, glossary,
photographs, and illustrations.

144 Clifford, Martin. <u>Microphones: How They Work and
How to Use Them.</u> Blue Ridge Summit, Pa.: TAB
Books, 1977. 224 pp.

Considers sound in the studio, in public address
situations, or in the home. Chapters deal with the
world of sound, meet the mike, microphone patterns,
characteristics of microphones, use with musical instruments, voice use, and special applications. Aimed
at the non-expert in the field. Photographs, glossary,
and index.

145 Gifford, F. <u>Tape: A Radio News Handbook.</u> New
York: Hastings House Publishers, 1977. 224 pp.

This comprehensive guide to using tape in radio
news is a valuable reference for anyone working with
any form of tape as well as those involved with radio
news. Such basic information as splicing, dubbing,

and tape editing are covered. Sections include such
areas as telephone tape, broadcast tape forms and
contents, writing for tape, etc. Photographs, appendixes, glossary and index.

146 Gross, Lynne S. Self Instruction in Radio Production.
     Los Alamitos, Calif.: Hwong Publishing Company,
     1976. 116 pp.

This book is a "cookbook" of exercises which students are to complete in order to gain knowledge of
radio production. The first half of the book contains
point by point directions to lead students to the com-
pletion of the exercises. The second half is programmed materials on elementary audio theory. Graphs
and illustrations.

147 McLeish, Robert. The Techniques of Radio Production.
     New York: Focal Press/Hastings House, 1979. 297
     pp.

Gives information in equipment, microphones, turn-
tables, tape recorders, discs, tape editing, patching,
cueing microphone setups and all other areas that are
essential in putting together a radio program. Diagrams, illustrations, and further readings.

148 Nisbett, Alec. The Technique of the Sound Studio: Ra-
     dio, Television, Recording. 4th revised edition. New
     York: Hastings House Publishers/Focal Press, 1979.
     560 pp.

A valuable book for the small film producer, news-
film cameraman and in-plant film worker who shoot
in sound. Describes procedures necessary to record
professional quality sound on tape or film. Discusses
sound from the simplest to the most complex sound
studio systems. Diagrams, glossary, illustrations,
and index.

149 Overman, Michael. Understanding Sound, Video and Film
     Recording. Blue Ridge Summit, Pa.: TAB Books,
     1978. 142 pp.

Analysis of the history, theory, practice and hardware of recording and reproducing sound and pictures
on cylinders, discs, films, and tapes. Explains the

theory behind both audio and video recording. Gives
an insight into the technical evolution of recording
instruments. Good reference. Illustrations and index.

150 Woram, John M. The Recording Studio Handbook. Plain-
view, New York: Sagamore Publishing Company,
1976. 496 pp.

Includes chapters on the decibel, sound, microphone design, microphone technique, loudspeakers,
echo, reverberation, equalizers, magnetic recording
tape, studio noise reduction systems, and the list
goes on. Good reference. Appendixes, bibliography,
glossary, photographs, and diagrams.

B. TELEVISION

See also no. 222.

151 Arlen, Michael J. Thirty Seconds. New York: Farrar,
Straus and Giroux, 1980. 211 pp.

A book on making a television commercial for
AT&T. It is a well written and amusing case study
about the actual business of commercial message
creation. This book will appeal to both general
viewers of television and to more sophisticated students of the TV medium.

152 Atienza, Loretta J. VTR Workshop: Small Format Video. New York: UNIPUB, 1977. 114 pp.

This monograph is one of a series on communication technology and utilization. It discusses the
operations and applications of small format video
taping. This monograph has direct relevance for development workers, communications and project support personnel in the developing world. Other mono-
graphs in the series include the following: Super 8:
The Modest Medium; Film Animation: A Simplified
Approach; Audio Cassettes; and The User Medium.
Photographs, illustrations, appendix, glossary, bibliography, and index.

153 Burrows, Thomas D. , and Donald N. Wood. Television

Production Disciplines and Techniques. Dubuque,
Iowa: Wm. C. Brown Company, 1978. 358 pp.

Designed as a basic, introductory text for a college course in TV production. Well illustrated and
useful text for beginning production course. Photographs, illustrations, appendix, glossary, bibliography,
and index.

154 Busch, H. Ted, and Terry Landeck. The Making of a
Television Commercial. New York: Macmillan Publishing Company, 1980. 175 pp.

The behind the scenes details of arranging, planning, and shooting the modern TV commercial are
portrayed with dialogue, camera and action.

155 Carroll, J. A. , and R. E. Sherriffs. TV Lighting Handbook. Blue Ridge Summit, Pa.: TAB Books, 1977.
226 pp.

This book is designed to train technicians and ac-
quaint producers, directors, and anyone in production
with the basics and specifics of TV lighting. In workbook format, the reader learns to design lighting setups for all types of productions, indoors as well as
outdoors, for both color and black and white TV. Illustrations, photographs, and index.

156 Combes, Peter, and John Tiffin. Television Production
for Education. New York: Focal Press, Inc. (Hastings House), 1978. 192 pp.

Handbook for students training as educational television producers and directors. Contents include
Characteristics of TV Systems; Technical, Practical,
and Resource Limitations; Design of Shots, Lighting,
Floor Plans; VTR Editing. Diagrams and photographs.

157 Englander, A. Arthur, and Paul Petzold. Filming for
Television. New York: Focal Press, Inc. , 1976.
226 pp.

A knowledgeable examination of the contribution
film can make to television; of its ability to meet the
restraints imposed by time, by economics, by the
weather; of its flexibility in a variety of contexts.
Diagrams, photographs, and glossary.

158 Gradus, Ben. Directing: The Television Commercial.
     New York: Hastings House Publishers, 1981. 236
     pp.

        Written by a top director of commercials and TV
     documentaries. This book is both a guide to techniques
     for and a study of the philosophy of the director of
     television commercials. It is geared towards the stu-
     dent and beginning professional, and will prove useful
     to veteran directors who want to review the field and
     acquire some new insights and techniques. Appendix,
     index, and photographs.

159 McCavitt, William E. Television Studio Operations Man-
     ual. Revised 1980 edition. Indiana, Pa.: A. G.
     Halldin Publishing, 1980. 104 pp.

        Basic manual for beginners in television produc-
     tion. Includes responsibilities for each position in a
     production team, script writing, and set design. Pho-
     tographs, illustrations, and bibliographies.

160 Millerson, Gerald. The Technique of Television Produc-
     tion. 10th revised edition. New York: Hastings
     House Publishers, 1979. 365 pp.

        One of the best standard guides to the overall pro-
     duction process, this offers more than 1100 diagrams
     to supplement the detailed text. Illustrations, bibliog-
     raphy, and diagrams.

161 Mitchell, Wanda B. , and James D. Kirkham. Televising
     Your Message: Producing Effective Television Com-
     munication. Skokie, Ill.: National Textbook Company,
     1981. 231 pp.

        Another textbook aimed at the public school market.
     Covers television production, as well as the persua-
     sive and communicative elements of television. Index,
     glossary, photographs, appendix, and illustrations.

162 Paulson, Robert C. ENG/Field Production Handbook:
     Guide to Using Mini Video Equipment. New York:
     Broadband Information Service, Inc. , 1976. 163 pp.

        A guide to using mini video equipment as the au-
     thor describes the book. Full of a lot of good infor-

mation concerning field production and equipment man-
ufactured for this purpose. Illustrations, photographs,
and graphs.

163   Stasheff, Edward; Rudy Bretz; John Gartley; and Lynn
Gartley.   The Television Program: Its Direction and
Production.   5th edition.   New York: Hill and Wang,
1976.   243 pp.

Provides information on the production and direction of television programs.   Includes the television
studio, control room, terms, shots and lenses, composition and other basic information needed for television production.   One chapter on non-broadcast television is also included.   Index, photographs, charts,
and figures.

164   Utz, Peter.   Video User's Handbook.   Englewood Cliffs,
N. J. :   Prentice-Hall Publishers, 1980.   410 pp.

Written in terms that both the layman and the professionals can understand.   Covers all aspects of television production for use in home, industry, education and professional uses.   Some topics covered are
receivers, videotape players/recorders, cameras,
switchers, lighting, audio, graphics, editing, and port-
able equipment.   An informative and useful tool.   Appendixes, bibliography, index, illustrations, photographs, and charts.

165   Wardwell, Douglas.   Television Production Handbook.
Blue Ridge Summit, Pa. :   TAB Books, Inc. , 1981.
302 pp.

Covers the standard areas for such a book including the TV Management/Production team, camera
shots and lenses, shot composition, lighting, make-
up, directing, electronic editing, and more.   Index.

166   Wicking, Christopher, and Tise Vahimagi.   The American Vein: Directors and Directions in Television.
New York: E. P. Dutton Company, 1979.   261 pp.

This is a reference book on film in television.   It
is the first comprehensive work to consider films that
have been made especially for the small screen, either
as TV movies or as series segments.   It classifies

them under the names of the people who created them.
Index and appendix.

167 Wilke, Bernard. Creating Special Effects for TV and
     Films. New York: Focal Press, Inc. , 1977. 158
     pp.

     A basic guide to the design and use of special ef-
     fects and props in film and television production. Dia-
     grams, glossary, and further readings.

168 Wurtzel, Alan. Television Production. New York: Mc-
     Graw-Hill Company, 1979. 624 pp.

     The most current, comprehensive book available
     at the date of its publication. The book covers, in
     detail, the technical and aesthetic aspects of tele-
     vision production at all levels, from closed circuit
     operations, to small and medium stations, to sophis-
     ticated network productions. A highly recommended
     text for courses in television production. Glossary,
     index, photographs, and charts.

C. WRITING

See also nos. 401, 402.

169 Blum, Richard A. Television Writing from Concept to
     Contract. New York: Hastings House, 1980. 184
     pp.

     Details both the business and process of writ-
     ing for both commercial and public television.
     Covers all aspects of writing for television. The
     process of selling a new script is covered also. A
     good resource for writers, teachers and students of
     TV and film writing. Appendix, annotated bibliog-
     raphy, index, and graphs.

170 Brady, Ben. The Keys to Writing for Television and
     Film. 3rd edition. Dubuque, Iowa: Kendall/Hunt
     Publishing, 1978. 281 pp.

     Good book for beginning writing class. Purpose
     is strictly for TV and film dramatic writing as op-
     posed to writing for news. Written by a professional,

it gives a good insight into the problems of writing
and uses many script examples for illustrations.
Writing for radio is not included.   Appendix, glossary,
and index.

171   Brenner, Alfred.   The TV Scriptwriter's Handbook.   Cincinnati, Ohio: Writer's Digest Books, 1980.   320 pp.

Focus is on the dramatic form with chapters on
the new writer, the plot, the producer and editor, the
premise, story conferences, dramatic construction,
character and more.   Would serve as a very satisfac-
tory textbook.   Appendixes.

172   Coe, Michelle E.   How to Write for Television.   New
York: Crown Publishers, 1980.   150 pp.

Contains 45 mini-chapters averaging three pages
each, including commercials, interviews, narratives,
etc.

173   Lee, Robert, and Robert Misiorowski.   Script Models:
A Handbook for the Media Writer.   New York: Hastings House, 1978.   96 pp.

A resource book for the beginning writer interested
in radio, television or film.   This book consists of
mostly sample scripts and should be used with a more
comprehensive text on writing for these various media.
Glossary, readings for writer's books and periodicals.

174   Maloney, Martin, and Paul Max Rubenstein.   Writing for
the Media.   Englewood Cliffs, N. J. :   Prentice-Hall
Publishing Company, 1980.   293 pp.

This is a book about writing for the media.   Some
rather specialized kinds of writing created by the demands of still photography, motion picture photography,
and audio and visual recording techniques.   A six-part
appendix deals with the writer's qualifications, a glossary of terms, a selling proposal, a treatment for a
television pilot script, a television documentary script
and a treatment for an industrial film.   Good book for
the beginner.   Index, appendix, and glossary.

175   Miller, William.   Screenwriting for Narrative Film and
Television.   New York: Hastings House, 1980.   256
pp.

Chapters deal with the writer as creator and craftsman, narrative structure, selected narrative techniques, characters and how to describe them, the comedy format, adaptation, etc. Appendixes and glossary.

176   Willis, Edgar E.   Writing Scripts for Television, Radio and Film.   New York: Holt, Rinehart and Winston, 1981.   322 pp.

Review of Willis' 1967 work on radio/television. The book covers all aspects of writing for broadcast and film, including commercials, variety, education, special events, drama, minority and ethnic programs, comedy, and the list goes on.   Index and bibliography.

D.   PERFORMANCE

177   Fridell, Squire.   Acting in Television Commercials for Fun and Profit.   New York: Crown Publishing, 1980. 165 pp.

Divided into sections on "Before the Agent" and "After the Agent." First part includes photographs as needed, résumé, schools, unions, and the agents. The second gets into the actual process of the system and the money.   Appendixes.

178   Hawes, William.   The Performer in Mass Media: In Media Professions and in the Community.   New York: Hastings House Publishers, 1978.   352 pp.

Comprehensive guide to everything beginning performers need to know to present themselves in the most professional manner possible in any mass media. Appearance, voice, movement, the technical aspects of mass media performing are some of the subjects covered.   Illustrations, make-up color chart, glossary, notes, resource list, bibliography, and index.

179   Hindman, James; Larry Kirkman; and Elizabeth Monk. TV Acting: A Manual for Camera Performance.   New York: Hastings House, 1979.   191 pp.

Explores the technical reality of TV and provides

a basic understanding of and vocabulary for television. The book explains ways of doing things simply and correctly, provides a broad understanding of why and how things are done in television production. Index, bibliography, and illustrations.

180   Hyde, Stuart. <u>Television and Radio Announcing.</u>   3rd edition.   Boston: Houghton Mifflin, 1979.   467 pp.

Presents new language and English language usage chapters.   New sections also cover preparation, production and performance for various kinds of announcing.   The sections on voice and diction, music announcing, and sports announcing have been expanded.   Index, glossary, and photographs.

E.   GENERAL

181   Herdeg, Walter, editor.   <u>Film and TV Graphic 2:   An International Survey of the Art of Film Animation.</u>   New York: Hastings House Publishers, 1976.   212 pp.

Provides a thorough and international examination of all essential aspects of film and TV graphics and their design.

182   Ravage, John W.   <u>Television: The Director's Viewpoint.</u>   Boulder, Colo.:   Westview Press, 1978.   184 pp.

A study of the role of the director in the producer-dominated medium of commercial television.   Includes interviews with twelve of the leading directors of commercial programs.   The book also analyzes the major issues facing television, its past, its present, and the audience that watches.   Index and glossary.

183   Ray, Sidney F.   <u>The Lens in Action.</u>   New York: Focal Press, Inc., 1976.   160 pp.

Combines a review of the state of the art of lens design with a survey of modern lenses and their applications.   The limits of specific lens design and the requirements for special lenses are discussed.   Diagrams, glossary, and further readings.

184   Rowlands, Avril Joyce.   <u>Script Continuity and the Pro-</u>

duction Secretary: In Film and TV. New York: Hastings
House Publishers/Focal Press, Inc. , 1977.   184 pp.

Explains exactly what a continuity person does and
shows how important the role is in making a film.
Illustrations, glossary, and further readings.

7. NEWS

A. INTERVIEWING

185 Brady, John. The Craft of Interviewing. Cincinnati, Ohio: Writer's Digest, 1976. 244 pp.

An informative guide for both print and broadcast journalists on when, why, and how to ask the right questions; written by the editor of Writer's Digest. A good book on asking questions for both beginners and veteran interviewers. Index.

186 Broughton, Irv. The Art of Interviewing for Television, Radio and Film. Blue Ridge Summit, Pa.: TAB Books, 1979. 266 pp.

Tells how to plan, prepare and conduct a film, video or radio interview for any purpose. This is a book of problem solving techniques that distill the essence of which good interviews are made. Illustrations and index.

187 Metzler, Ken. Creative Interviewing: The Writer's Guide to Gathering Information by Asking Questions. Englewood Cliffs, N.J.: Prentice-Hall, 1977. 174 pp.

Based on the belief of the author that journalism students lack the necessary skills to conduct good interviews. It covers various types of interviews including multiple interviews, the personality interview, and interviewing for broadcast. Special problems are also discussed, such as taking notes, using a tape recorder, the news conference, etc. Good reference and possible text for reporters, regardless of the media. Index, bibliography, and appendix.

B. WRITING

188   Altheide, David. Creating Reality: How TV News Dis-
      torts Events. Beverly Hills, Calif.: Sage Publica-
      tions, 1976. 228 pp.

      This work shows how the daily routine of news
      show production contributes to the distortion of re-
      ported events. Altheide compares local and national
      news sources, work routines and presentations to ar-
      gue that events become news because of the news
      perspective, not due to any objective characteristics.
      Appendix and references.

189   Bliss, Edward, Jr. , and John M. Patterson. Writing News
      for Broadcast. 2nd edition, fully revised. New York:
      Columbia University Press, 1978. 220 pp.

      A definitive text for teaching news writing for radio
      and television. The fully revised edition includes new
      sections on innovations in broadcast journalism; among
      them "New Minutes" and "On the Road" segments--and
      more than 40 new examples of news writing. Bibliog-
      raphy and index.

190   Hall, Mark W. Broadcast Journalism: An Introduction
      to News Writing. 2nd edition, revised. New York:
      Hastings House Publishers, 1978. 160 pp.

      This book provides the basic tools and effective
      guidelines for the presentation of news on both radio
      and television. This revised edition includes new
      chapters on journalistic rights and responsibilities,
      the mini-documentary and updated material through-
      out. Appendixes and index.

191   Hood, James R. , and Brad Kalbfeld, editors. The As-
      sociated Press Broadcast News Handbook. New York:
      Associated Press, 1981. 298 pp.

      According to the editors, this is the industry's
      most comprehensive look at the theory and practice
      of good broadcast news writing. It provides text on
      the basics of good writing with a dictionary-like guide
      to the specifics of broadcast style. Provides informa-
      tion on current usage, spelling and pronunciation of
      thousands of words and phrases. Excellent reference
      for the news person.

192   Hunter, Julius; Lynn S. Gross. Broadcast News: The
      Inside Out. St. Louis, Mo.: C. V. Mosby Company,
      1980. 363 pp.

         This text offers a broad, hands-on approach to
      modern newscasting. Chapters discuss such topics
      as equipment, facilities, personnel, types of news,
      writing and editing. The authors also include com-
      plete, up-to-date coverage of the FCC. Illustrations,
      teacher's guide, test manual, glossary, appendix, and
      photographs.

193   Mencher, Melvin. News Reporting and Writing. 2nd
      edition. Dubuque, Iowa: Wm. C. Brown Publishers,
      1981. 634 pp.

         This basic journalism text emphasizes reporting
      and writing. Interviewing, reporter ethics, feature
      writing, broadcast journalism, poll assessment and
      laws affecting reporters are covered in this edition,
      along with basic aspects of journalism. The section
      on broadcast writing has also been expanded in this
      edition. Index, photographs, figures, and tables.

194   Smeyak, Paul. Broadcast News Writing. Columbus,
      Ohio: Grid Publishing Company, 1977. 202 pp.

         This text was designed to help students get in-
      volved in the writing process. As a method of in-
      struction, broadcast news stories are examined in
      four parts: lead, organization, grammar, and style.
      The experienced news writer, who writes by instinct,
      might cringe at this learning device, but it supposedly
      will help the novice writer to examine the four ele-
      ments of a news story and put them together into an
      acceptable writing style. Appendixes, photographs,
      and illustration.

195   Stephens, Mitchell. Broadcast News: Radio Journalism
      and an Introduction to Television. New York: Holt,
      Rinehart & Winston, 1980. 301 pp.

         The first three parts of this book deal with both
      basic writing and reporting skills for radio and tele-
      vision. Specific techniques and examples are drawn
      from radio news. Part four introduces the somewhat
      more advanced skills specific to television news. Deals

with both small town and big city journalists.   Index,
photographs, illustrations, and bibliography.

C.   POLITICAL

See also nos.   104, 105, 106, 112, 113, 114, 116, 120, 282.

196   Braestrup, Peter.   Big Story: How the American Press
      and Television Reported and Interpreted the Crisis of
      TET, 1968, in Vietnam and Washington.   Volume 1.
      Boulder, Colo.:   Westview Press, 1977.   740 pp.

      Using TET as a case history in depth of the por-
      trayal of the war in Vietnam, the author has compiled
      a remarkable document that reflects the analysis of
      millions of words published in newspapers and news
      magazines and broadcast over radio and television;
      the examination of thousands of feet of TV film; and
      interviews with scores of participants in Vietnam.
      Continued in Volume 2 below.   Graphs, photographs,
      and index.

197   Braestrup, Peter.   Big Story: How the American Press
      and Television Reported and Interpreted the Crisis of
      TET, 1968, in Vietnam and Washington.   Volume 2.
      Boulder, Colo.:   Westview Press, 1977.   698 pp.

      Continuation of Volume 1 above concerning the
      TET crisis in Vietnam in 1968.   Index and appendixes.

198   Gitlin, Todd.   The Whole World Is Watching: Mass Me-
      dia in the Making and Unmaking of the New Left.
      Berkeley, Calif.:   University of California Press,
      1980.   327 pp.

      Focusing upon the case of Students for a Demo-
      cratic Society, the author explores the ways in which
      journalist framing conventions combined to sustain and
      advance elite interests so effectively that repression
      through overt censorship was seldom invoked in cov-
      erage of New Left activities by national news organi-
      zations.

199   Paletz, David L., and Robert M. Entman.   Media Power
      Politics.   New York: Free Press, 1981.   310 pp.

      Uses a number of case studies, including the 1976

and 1980 presidential campaigns, various congressional investigations, Watergate, and how different presidents have been covered in the press, to show how the media dictates public opinion and thus affects political reality in the United States. Bibliography and index.

200 Ranney, Austin, editor. The Past and Future of Presidential Debates. Washington, D. C. : American Enterprise Institute for Public Policy Research, 1979. 226 pp.

Review of the 1960 and 1976 efforts, along with material on development of Section 315 legislation. GOP and Democratic views of the 1976 faceoffs, and essays both in favor of and against such political media use.

201 Spragens, William C. The Presidency and the Mass Media in the Age of Television. Washington, D. C. : University Press of America, 1978. 425 pp.

This book is an up-to-date analysis of the relationship between the White House and the Washington Correspondent Corps. It traces the development of this relationship and gives a functional analysis of both institutions. Index.

D. GENERAL

202 Bittner, John R. , and Denise A. Bittner. Radio Journalism. Englewood Cliffs, N. J. : Prentice-Hall, Inc. , 1977. 207 pp.

Offers thorough coverage of many areas, from how to obtain your job, and how to gather and deliver the news, to how to build mini-documentaries and news features. It shows you how to conduct interviews and how to make the local radio news as professional as network radio news. Index and appendix.

203 Denniston, Lyle W. The Reporter and the Law: Techniques of Covering the Courts. New York: Hastings House Publishers, 1980. 288 pp.

Discusses the day-to-day techniques of news reporting of the courts which provides an important ex-

planation of the key differences between the professions of journalism and the law. The book does not
tell neophyte reporters how to cover the courts, but
it does provide helpful background in that specialized
field. Bibliography and index.

204 Harris, Morgan, and Patti Karp. How to Make News
     and Influence People. Blue Ridge Summit, Pa.:
     TAB Books, 1976. 140 pp.

     This is a guidebook for gaining publicity on radio,
     TV, newspaper, etc. Tells how to plan publicity pro-
     grams, organize materials and equipment, develop
     reliable contacts in the media, write promotional copy,
     preface stories and releases. Index and bibliography.

205 Hulteng, John L. The News Media: What Makes Them
     Tick. Englewood Cliffs, N.J.: Prentice-Hall, Inc.,
     1979. 166 pp.

     Analysis of the forces, traditions, influences, and
     pressures that determine how the media function.
     Relationships among the various media and other
     segments of society are critically analyzed. The
     inner workings of the media themselves are probed
     to determine what stresses, values, and motivations
     dictate the perceptions of reality passed on to the
     public by the media. Index and readings.

206 Rather, Dan. The Camera Never Blinks. New York:
     Ballantine Books, 1977. 320 pp.

     The author offers his own insights into such vital sub-
     jects as checkbook journalism; the demands made by
     government officials that reporters expose their
     sources, as exemplified by the Daniel Schorr Case;
     and the dangers posed by the celebrity syndrome
     when the news business becomes show business.
     With immediacy, humor and an eye for the revealing
     incident and colorful detail, Rather tells the behind-
     the-scene stories of recent history's stormiest events.
     Index.

207 Smith, Anthony. Goodbye Gutenberg. New York: Ox-
     ford University Press, 1980. 367 pp.

     First analysis of the news realities of newspaper

publishing. Looks at the effects of computerization on the industry. The effects of other technology are also discussed. Part I looks at the Third Revolution in communication; Part II, the newspaper industry of the United States; and Part III, the New Media. Good look at a changing industry. Index, glossary, appendix, and figures.

208 Strentz, Herbert. News Reporters and News Sources: What Happens Before the Story Is Written? Ames, Iowa: Iowa University Press, 1978. 108 pp.

This book is about what happens before news stories are written. Content covers such areas as power of the press, pitfalls awaiting the reporter, news sources, and traditional and nontraditional news. Index.

8. ADVERTISING

A. CHILDREN

See also nos. 127, 131, 132.

209 Adler, Richard P.; Scott Ward; Gerald Lesser; Laurene Meringhoff; Thomas S. Robertson; and John R. Rossiter. The Effects of Television Advertising on Children. Lexington, Mass.: Lexington Books, 1980. 367 pp.

This book reviews the existing research on the effects of television advertising on children and recommends a plan for future research. The book's twelve chapters are organized around nine issues, followed by a review of current and proposed regulations on that issue, a review and evaluation of empirical research evidence and a summary. A good reference. Index, bibliography, appendix, and tables.

210 Robertson, Thomas S.; John R. Rossiter; and Terry C. Gleason. Televised Medicine: Advertising and Children. New York: Praeger Special Studies, 1979. 192 pp.

An assessment of the effects of medicine advertising on children, this book shows that children are exposed to medicine commercials despite the fact that such commercials are not directed at them and despite industry self-regulation codes.

211 Ward, Scott; Daniel Wackman; and Ellen Wartella. How Children Learn to Buy. Volume I. Beverly Hills, Calif.: Sage Publications, 1977. 272 pp.

This volume explores the issue of how children learn, or fail to learn, to become intelligent consumers. The authors investigate the benefits and

abuses of television advertising in order to identify
the influences that help or harm children who are
trying to understand how our consumer society operates.

B. PROMOTION

212 Gompertz, Rolf. Promotion and Publicity Handbook for
     Broadcasters. Blue Ridge Summit, Pa.: TAB Books,
     1977. 334 pp.

     A practical handbook for radio and TV station pub-
     licity and Public Relations departments. Planning a
     publicity campaign, tools of the trade, organizing,
     preparing, and disseminating a press kit are covered
     in the book. Included also is a list of press outlets.
     Photographs, graphs, and index.

C. GENERAL

213 Barnouw, Erik. The Sponsor: Notes on a Modern Po-
     tentate. New York: Oxford University Press, 1978.
     220 pp.

     In this book, Barnouw confronts the touchy, far-
     reaching issue of how the television industry has
     gradually meshed itself into the needs and wishes of
     sponsors--influencing programming, news and docu-
     mentaries, and shaping American culture, mores,
     and politics. Index and photographs.

214 Gilson, Christopher C., and Harold W. Berkman. Ad-
     vertising Concepts and Strategies. New York: Ran-
     dom House, 1980. 610 pp.

     This contemporary textbook gives a lively and clear
     account of basic advertising principles, offering many
     examples and a wide coverage of media and methods.

215 Jewler, A. Jerome. Creative Strategy in Advertising.
     Belmont, Calif.: Wadsworth Publishing Company,
     1981. 230 pp.

     Fifteen chapters dealing with the role of the ad-
     vertising copywriter, the various media, how to write

for them, creative presentations and employment opportunities.   Covers both print and electronic production.

216   Murphy, Jonne.   Handbook of Radio Advertising.   Rad-
      nor, Pa. :   Chilton Book Company, 1980.   240 pp.

      Designed to answer the needs of radio advertising.
      Includes such areas as national advertisers, retailers,
      advertising agencies, and case histories.   Index,
      charts, bibliography, and glossary.

217   Oglivy, David.   Confessions of an Advertising Man.
      New York: Ballantine Books, 1978.   152 pp.

      The complete forthright guide to the world of ad-
      vertising and advertising agencies.   Sample chapters
      include, How to Get Clients, How to Build Great Ad
      Campaigns, How to Write Potent Copy, How to Make
      Good Television Commercials, and Should Advertising
      Be Abolished?   Good discussion of the complex busi-
      ness of advertising.   Index.

218   Paletz, David L. ; Roberta E. Pearson; and Donald L.
      Willis.   Politics in Public Service Advertising on
      Television.   New York: Praeger Special Studies,
      1977.   123 pp.

      Part I of this comprehensive study of television's
      public service announcements describes how the main
      organizations involved in the decision-making process
      decides to grant some groups air time and refuse it
      to others.   Part II assesses the overall impact of the
      PSA on the American political system.   Finds the Ad-
      vertising Council and other "gatekeepers" of PSAs are
      not receptive to controversial groups and that PSAs
      tend to focus on the inadequacies of individuals rather
      than of government or institutions.

219   Sissors, Jack Z. , and E. R. Petray.   Advertising Media
      Planning.   Chicago: Crain Books, 1976.   341 pp.

      Introductory book on decision making about adver-
      tising media.   Suggests how to make the right deci-
      sions in choosing the right media to fulfill marketing
      objectives and strategies.   The book is both theoreti-
      cal and practical.   It is written for advertising ma-

jors, beginners in the media departments of advertising agencies, account executives or others in agencies, whose training has not been in media. The
book is divided into two general segments. The first
dealing with concepts and practices in planning. The
second deals with special problems that affect planning. Index, glossary, appendixes, selected readings,
charts, and graphs.

220 Ulanoff, Stanley M. Advertising in America: An Introduction to Persuasive Communication. New York:
Hastings House Publishers, 1977. 512 pp.

A survey text covering the entire field of advertising from the viewpoint of methods, management
and media. Illustrations and examples of current
mass media advertising are given. Illustrations.

221 Wademan, Victor. Money-Making Advertising: A Guide
to Advertising That Sells. New York: Wiley. 1981.
142 pp.

A well-illustrated text on how to design and recognize effective ads, both for print and broadcast media.

222 White, Hooper. How to Produce an Effective TV Commercial. Chicago: Crain Books, 1981. 305 pp.

Step-by-step process of producing a commercial.
Included are chapters on preparing the idea, pricing
the commercial, producing it, post-production, casting, film vs. tape, producing on location or on a set,
music, producing live action, animation and the role
of computers and other special effects. Glossary,
index, and illustrations.

223 Zeigler, Sherilyn K., and Herbert H. Howard. Broadcast Advertising: A Comprehensive Working Textbook. Columbus, Ohio: Grid Publishing, 1978. 341
pp.

Deals with all aspects of broadcast advertising, both
radio and television; discusses such areas as the regulations of broadcast advertising, audiences, writing,
testing and production. Good workbook for advertising
students. Includes suggested readings, questions and
assignments. Index, notes, photographs, and exhibits.

9. MINORITIES

224 Butler, Matilda, and William Paisley. <u>Women and the</u>
<u>Mass Media: A Source Book for Research and Ac-</u>
<u>tion.</u> New York: Human Sciences Press, 1980. 432
pp.

The book is divided into five sections ranging from
an overview of the history of women's rights in America to a discussion of sexism in language and image.
The authors focus on possible changes of the image
of women through broadcasting, the media licensed by
the government.

225 Ceulemans, Mieke, and Guido Fauconnier. <u>Mass Media:</u>
<u>The Image, Role, and Social Conditions of Women:</u>
<u>A Collection and Analysis of Research Materials.</u>
New York: UNIPUB, 1979. 78 pp.

First section of this report deals with the image
of women in mass media throughout the world. The
second section deals with the professional status of
women in mass media. As one would expect, the
evidence presented indicates that media images tend
to define women within the narrow confines of their
traditional roles and their sexual appeal to men. The
research also shows that the media are male dominated and male oriented. References.

226 Dickerson, Nancy. <u>Among Those Present.</u> New York:
Ballantine Books, 1978. 280 pp.

The inside story of the first female national network news correspondent, her journalistic scoops and
her personal and professional relationships with four
American Presidents from Kennedy to Ford. Covers
Dickerson's 25 years as a journalist. Photographs.

227   Epstein, Laurily Keir, editor. Women and the News.
      New York: Hastings House, 1978. 192 pp.

          Collection of essays that discuss the current prob-
      lems concerning how the news media report about
      women and how they can be improved. Tables, bib-
      liography, and index.

228   Gelfman, Judith S. Women in Television News. New
      York: Columbia University Press, 1976. 186 pp.

          The author has based her findings on interviews
      and on-the-job observations of thirty women who have
      succeeded in television news. Some topics covered
      include: background for a career, being a woman in
      television news, career versus home life, career
      guidance and advice. Bibliography and index.

229   Marzolf, Marion. Up from the Footnote: A History of
      Women Journalists. New York: Hastings House Pub-
      lishers, 1977. 310 pp.

          A look at women journalists in newspapers, news
      magazines, radio and television from colonial printers
      to anchorwomen. Index.

230   Miller, Randall N. , editor. Ethnic Images in American
      Film and Television. Philadelphia: Balch Institute,
      1978. 173 pp.

          Eight sections, each dealing with different ethnic
      groups. Section one is devoted to blacks; section
      two, Jews; section three, Germans; section four,
      Irish; section five, Italians; section six, Polish; sec-
      tion seven, Puerto Ricans; and section eight, Asians.
      Each looks at how both film and television have treat-
      ed these various ethnic groups.

231   Noble, Gil. Black Is the Color of My TV Tube. Sea-
      caucus, N. J. : Lyle Stuart, Inc. , 1981.

          Traces the author's professional career in broad-
      casting and describes how the media has failed to hire
      blacks in meaningful positions. One of the few books
      available on blacks in broadcasting.

232   Rubin, Bernard, editor. Small Voices and Great Trum-

pets: Minorities and the Media. New York: Praeger Publishers, 1980. 308 pp.

This book deals with the failures of the news media in their coverage of minorities as well as the
ethnic imbalance of the staffs doing the coverage.

233 Tuchman, Gaye; Arlene Kaplan Daniels; and James Benet,
editors. Hearth and Home: Images of Women in the
Mass Media. New York: Oxford University Press,
1978. 335 pp.

Examines the sex-role stereotype in the media.
Reports on the findings of social science researchers
who, under a grant from the National Science Foundation, have examined television, women's magazines,
and the women's pages of newspapers to determine the
effects of the mass media upon women. Through systematic and consistent review of findings, the work
ultimately addresses the question of how the media
can be changed to free women from the tyranny of
both overt and covert messages that would limit their
lives to hearth and home. Index, references, annotated bibliography, and tables.

10.   RESPONSIBILITY

See also nos. 28, 272, 307, 308.

234   Casebier, Allan, and Janet Jenks Casebier. Social Responsibilities of the Mass Media. Washington, D. C.: University Press of America, 1978.   260 pp.

Revised and edited proceeding of a 1976 conference sponsored by the University of Southern California on the subject of social responsibilities of the mass media.   Contributors are nationally known scholars, philosophers, media figures, and social scientists. Bibliography.

235   Cirino, Robert. Don't Blame the People. New York: Vintage Books, 1978.   339 pp.

A documented account of how the news media use bias, distortion and censorship to manipulate public opinion.   Tables, appendix, notes, and index.

236   Cowen, Geoffrey. See No Evil: The Backstage Battle over Sex and Violence on Television. New York: Simon and Schuster, 1978.   313 pp.

Cowen, the lawyer credited with successfully challenging the family hour restrictions on TV content, traces the history of that confrontation.   He reveals the battles at every level of all three networks over the sex and violence guidelines.

237   Cullen, Maurice R. Mass Media and the First Amendment. Dubuque, Iowa: Wm. C. Brown, 1981.   450 pp.

Introduction to such topics as historical background of the First Amendment, mass media responsibility, reporting the news, mass media audiences, the courts, controls over sex on the media, media ethics, and more.   Index and bibliography.

238   Rivers, William L.; Wilbur Schramm; and Clifford G.
      Christians.   Responsibility in Mass Communication.
      3rd edition.   New York: Harper and Row, 1980.
      378 pp.

      The third edition of this text on media ethics in-
      cludes the same stress on responsible behavior for
      professional journalists as its two predecessors.   The
      authors have updated their materials, using recent
      figures, events, and illustrations.   Appendix.

11. SOCIETY

A. ROLE OF TELEVISION

See also nos. 27, 97, 209, 210, 211, 218, 280, 282, 285, 305, 306, 310.

239 Adler, Richard, editor. Understanding Television: Essays on Television as a Social and Cultural Force. New York: Praeger Publisher, 1981. 456 pp.

Analyzes TV news, comic and dramatic programs, the state of TV criticism and new developments in the medium. The book examines TV's impact and potential. Index.

240 Belson, William. Television Violence and the Adolescent Boy. Lexington, Mass.: Lexington Books, 1978. 529 pp.

In this book the author describes the techniques he developed to measure the effects on adolescent boys on exposure to television violence. The book includes the complete findings of the study, a commentary on the implications of the findings and recommendations. Notes, tables, figures, references, and bibliography.

241 Berger, Arthur Asa. Television as an Instrument of Terror: Essays on Media, Popular Culture and Everyday Life. New Brunswick, N.J.: Transaction Books, 1980. 214 pp.

The title is rather misleading since the book has essays not only on television but also on comics, advertising, humor, fads, stereotyping, etc. Interesting book, but don't look for terrorist activities here.

242 Comstock, George. Television in America. Beverly Hills, Calif.: Sage Publications, Inc., 1980. 160 pp.

Analyzes the impact of three decades of TV on American society. Shows evidence by a host of researchers--sociologists, social psychologists, political behavioralists, psychologists, journalists, and other mass communication researchers--to synthesize in this brief textbook what we currently know about our most powerful mass medium.

243 Coppa, Frank J. , editor. Screen and Society: The Impact of Television upon Aspects of Contemporary Civilization. Chicago: Nelson-Hall, 1979. 217 pp.

The questions addressed in this book are How has TV changed the educational and political process? How has it affected attendance at movies, theaters and sporting events? How has it influenced the urban crisis? How and to what extent has it altered popular culture and taste? How does public TV differ from commercial TV in the U. S. and abroad? The book does not provide definitive answers to these questions. However, it exposes some of the false generalizations about the medium; explores some of the newer developments; explores TV's impact in particular areas; and reviews the findings of a number of specialized studies, revealing their broad scope implications. Index and bibliography.

244 Goethals, Gregor T. The TV Ritual: Worship at the Video Altar. Boston: Beacon Press, 1981. 164 pp.

Informal discussion of the impact of television on American life by looking at selected programs.

245 Moody, Kate. Growing Up on Television: The TV Effect. New York: Time Books, 1980. 242 pp.

Chapters on growing up with TV, the physical effects, impact on learning and perception, effects on reading, etc. Discusses what action can be taken at home, at school, and by the general public. Appendixes.

246 Morgenstern, Steve, editor. Inside the TV Business. New York: Sterling Publishing Company, 1979. 223 pp.

This book gives insights into the explorations of the

conflicts and cooperation which shape what finally appears on the home TV screen. The authors are all top people in their specialties, including the heads of programming, children's programming, sports and news at the network level. Good look at the business. Index.

247 Ploghoft, Milton E. , and James A. Anderson. Education for the Television Age. Athens, Ohio: Cooperative Center for Social Sciences Education, 1981. 183 pp.

The proceedings of a national conference on the subject of Children and Television held in Philadelphia in 1979 is the topic of this book. Topics include elementary and secondary viewing skill projects, network and association activities, effects of critical viewing skill curriculums. Good reading for educators.

248 Sklar, Robert. Prime Time America: Life On and Behind the Television Screen. New York: Oxford University Press, 1980. 200 pp.

This book is a collection of the author's essays on the state of the art. Most of these essays were written in the mid-seventies and are not as relevant as they might have been once.

249 Williams, Frederick; Robert LaRose; and Frederica Frost. Children, Television, and Sex-Role Stereotyping. New York: Praeger Publishers, 1981. 160 pp.

A social-psychological assessment of the effects of television viewing on the development of sex-role stereotypes in children. Should provide a useful resource for scholars of sex-role development or television and children. Index.

250 Winick, Mariann, and Charles Winick. The Television Experience: What Children See. Beverly Hills, Calif. : Sage Publications, 1979. 224 pp.

Describes how children talk about television people and events. Provides the readers with a firsthand account of how children see the world of TV.

251 Witney, Steven, and Ronald P. Abeles. Television and
     Social Behavior: Beyond Violence and Children.
     Hillsdale, N. J. : Lawrence Erlbaum Association, 1981.
     356 pp.

     Thirteen original articles including the nature and
     effects of mass media, television research, organiza-
     tional perspective on television, social influences and
     television, influence of television on personal decision
     making, television and Afro-Americans, and more.
     Comprehensive, stimulating, and current by authors
     and consultants who are experts in this aspect of re-
     search.   Appendixes and index.

B.   GENERAL

252 Abel, Elie, editor. What's News: The Media in Ameri-
     can Society.   San Francisco: Institute for Contem-
     porary Studies, 1981. 296 pp.

     Probes such issues as the impact on journalists
     of the economic and political environments and pres-
     sures under which they work, the biases of news re-
     porters, and media accountability. Twelve distinguish-
     ed scholars, journalists, and media watchers point up
     both popular and professional misconceptions about the
     media.   Index and references.

253 Altheide, David L. , and Robert P. Snow.   Media Logic.
     Beverly Hills, Calif. : Sage Publications, 1979.   256
     pp.

     The authors suggest some conceptually fruitful ways
     of discovering and understanding the role of media in
     our lives.   They offer an analysis of social institu-
     tions transformed through media to illustrate not only
     how the logics and forms of media perspectives have
     transformed much of the social stock of knowledge we
     share, but also how any effort to single out particular
     "variables" of media impact is likely to miss the most
     fundamental reality of our social culture shaped by
     media.   Bibliography.

254 Atwan, Robert; Barry Orton; and William Vesterman,
     editors. American Mass Media: Industries and Is-
     sues. New York: Random House, 1978.   475 pp.

As the title indicates, this collection of articles addresses itself to two dominant features of American mass media: the industries that design and sustain each of the major channels of mass communications and the significant issues--social, political, and cul- tural--that shape and, in turn, have been shaped by these industries. Index, bibliography, illustrations, and photographs.

255 Bittner, John R. Professional Broadcasting: A Brief Introduction. Englewood Cliffs, N. J. : Prentice-Hall, Inc. , 1981. 255 pp.

Focuses on the field of professional broadcasting. This text concentrates on the contemporary operation and role of broadcasting in our society. The book is clearly written and well supported by illustrations. Index, glossary, bibliography, illustrations, and pho- tographs.

256 Cassata, Mary B. , and Molefi K. Asante. Mass Communi- cations Principles and Practices. Riverside, N. J. : Macmillan Publishing Company, 1979. 360 pp.

This attempts to present theories and practices of mass communication in order to explain how the vari- ous media influence society. Appendixes, glossary, bibliography, index, suggested readings, and instruc- tor's manual.

257 Davis, Dennis K. , and Stanley J. Baran. Mass Commu- nication and Everyday Life: A Perspective on Theory and Effects. Belmont, Calif. : Wadsworth Publishers, 1981. 250 pp.

This text focuses on how mass communications both contributes to and intrudes upon our lives. The text reviews the important controversies over mass com- munication influence for the past half century. Index.

258 Davis, Robert Edward. Response to Innovation: A Study of Popular Argument About New Mass Media. New York: Arno Press, 1976. 725 pp.

Though this book is only concerned with movies as one aspect of communications, the author has com- piled a great deal of valuable historical information on the attitudes toward the introduction of the motion picture, as well as radio and television.

259 Emery, Edwin, and Michael Emery. The Press and America: An Interpretative History of the Mass Media. 4th edition. Englewood Cliffs, N. J. : Prentice-Hall, Inc. , 1978. 173 pp.

Virtually every important issue of newspaper, radio and television journalism is covered in this edition. This fourth edition brings greater emphasis to the impact of the modern electronic media, including the use of TV in political campaigns, the Watergate era, the Vietnam war, and television's controversial social role in the 1960's and 70's. Illustrations.

260 Gumpert, Gary, and Robert Cathcart, editors. Inter/ Media: Interpersonal Communications in a Media World. New York: Oxford University Press, 1979. 600 pp.

A look at various media as they relate to interpersonal communication. This book emphasizes the point of view that everyone ought to be conscious of the influence that guides and structures our communication relationships. The purpose of the book is to provide insights into the awareness of the role of media in our daily environment. This is done through the use of essays on media and interpersonal communication by forty-one contributors. Bibliography.

261 Katz, Elihu. Social Research on Broadcasting: Proposals for Further Development. London: British Broadcasting Corporation, 1977. 116 pp.

The report was written on the basis of dozens of interviews during 1975 and 1976 with researchers, producers, and managers within the BBC, and academics in British universities; a variety of American academics and broadcast researchers; and a smattering of comparable professionals and scholars in other countries. The report was to present a number of detailed funding proposals for submission to foundations and other agencies. The report turns out to be more interesting and provocative than a simple collection of research proposals.

262 Kraus, Sidney, and Dennis Davis. The Effects of Mass
     Communications on Political Behavior. State College,
     Pa.: Pennsylvania State University Press, 1976.
     308 pp.

         Chapters relate mass communication to socializa-
     tion, the electoral process, political information, the
     political process, and the construction of political
     reality in society. Included also is an examination
     of methods of political communication research. Bib-
     liography and index.

263 McAnany, Emile; Jorge Schnitman; and Noreene Janus,
     editors. Communications and Social Structure: Criti-
     cal Studies in Mass Media Research. New York:
     Praeger Publishers, 1981. 352 pp.

         This book emphasizes the structure of the com-
     munications system which, to a large extent, deter-
     mines the content of the message sent. The editors
     have assembled twelve original contributions that ad-
     dress current critical issues facing international poli-
     cy makers, including the problems of changing the
     media from within, the structural constraints on re-
     forms of children's television and how advertising
     structure affects communication systems in countries
     other than the United States.

264 McCombs, Maxwell, and Lee Becker. Using Mass Com-
     munication Theory. Englewood Cliffs, N.J.: Pren-
     tice-Hall, Inc., 1979. 148 pp.

         This book offers a practical overview, based on
     investigation by social scientists in a variety of disci-
     plines, of the factual knowledge concerning the inter-
     action of mass communication and society. It is a
     concise introduction to messages for anyone seriously
     interested in communication.

265 Mander, Jerry. Four Arguments for the Elimination of
     Television. New York: William Morrow & Company,
     1978. 371 pp.

         A departure from previous writings about television,
     this book advocates that the medium is not reform-

able. Its problems are inherent in the technology itself and are so dangerous to personal health and sanity, to the environment, and to democratic process that TV ought to be eliminated forever. Bibliography.

266 Real, Michael R. Mass Mediated Culture. Englewood Cliffs, N. J.: Prentice-Hall, Inc., 1977. 289 pp.

This book draws on scholarship from many fields to create the first in-depth summary of the inter-action among mass media, popular culture, and life in contemporary society. The case studies investi-gate culture in the form of widespread patterns of be-lief and behavior as transmitted by media in all forms to large audiences. Good insight into the interna-tional system of mass-mediated culture that shapes life in English speaking countries. Index, bibliogra-phy, figures, and photographs.

267 Robinson, Glen O., editor. Communications for Tomor-row: Policy Perspectives for the 1980's. New York: Praeger Publishers, 1978. 512 pp.

To design a research and action program in com-munications, representatives from the communica-tions industry, government leaders and public advoca-cy leaders met under the auspices of the Aspen In-stitute to identify emergent communications issues and to assess their impact on society. Index, tables, and figures.

268 Sandman, Peter M.; David M. Rubin; and David B. Sach-man. Media Casebook: An Introductory Analysis of American Mass Communications. 2nd edition. Engle-wood Cliffs, N. J.: Prentice-Hall, Inc., 1976. 483 pp.

Significantly expanded, this revised edition probes functions, characteristics, and problems of the mass media in the United States. Each selection is a spe-cific example of the media at work, illustrating an important issue of media control, media process, or media coverage. Index.

269 Sellers, Leonard, and William L. Rivers, editors. Mass Media Issues: Articles and Commentaries. Engle-wood Cliffs, N. J.: Prentice-Hall, Inc., 1977. 370 pp.

An anthology with commentaries. Articles used present a broad view of mass media issues. The editors offer commentaries on the articles presented, supposedly a first in this type of text. Each of the mass media is explored as a social force. Constraints on the media are also examined. Good book for issues course in Mass Media Curriculum. Index and cartoons.

270 Stanley, Robert H. , and Charles S. Steinberg. The Media Environment: Mass Communication in American Society. New York: Hastings House, 1976. 306 pp.

A comprehensive survey examining the content, structure and control of the communications media and their impact on American society. Bibliography and index.

271 Stein, Ben. The View from Sunset Boulevard: America as Brought to You by the People Who Make Television. New York: Basic Books, 1979. 156 pp.

Behind-the-scenes look at television. Gives the reader insight into not only what goes into the making of a television show, but why. Not a production book but rather a think piece. Good reading for those interested in the field, as well as the general reading public. Index.

272 Stein, Jay W. Mass Media Education and a Better Society. Chicago: Nelson-Hall, Inc. , 1979. 164 pp.

Discusses the opposing positions of the two institutions (Education and Mass Media) and warns that they must find ways to join forces or face the possibility of canceling each other out as they cancel out the society they serve. The author suggests ways in which sophisticated communications systems can enhance the value and experience of public education and conversely how educators can apply their expertise to the upgrading of mass media fare. Index.

273 Tannebaum, Percy H. , editor. The Entertainment Functions of Television. Hillsdale, N. J. : Lawrence Eribaum Association, 1981. 262 pp.

The book consists of nine original papers including
such topics as news as entertainment, the power and
limitations of television, the effect of comedy on audiences, and more. Index.

274 Tunstall, Jeremy. The Media Are American. New York:
Columbia University Press, 1977. 352 pp.

Documents the global influence and impacts of Anglo-
American media. U. S. Government Policy, Madison
Avenue, the news, the movies, the alternatives to
Anglo-American domination of world media are a few
of the topics covered. Tables, references, bibliogra-
phy, and index.

275 Voelker, Francis, and Ludmila Voelker, editors. Mass
Media Forces in Our Society. 3rd edition. New
York: Harcourt Brace Jovanovich, Inc. , 1978. 470
pp.

Almost half of the 75 selections in the third edition are new. They represent a wide range of contemporary issues, writing styles, critical viewpoints,
and sources, from New West to The New Yorker.
Among the important new developments covered are
National Security vs. The First Amendment; women
in film; electronic newsgathering; trends in FM radio;
country music; and black journalism. Photographs,
illustrations, bibliography, index, and instructor's
manual.

276 Willener, Alfred; Guy Milliard; and Alex Gantry. Video-
logy and Utopia: Explorations in a New Medium.
Boston, Mass. : Routledge and Kegan Paul, 1976.
171 pp.

The authors draw on their experience working with
school children, teenagers, and a variety of cultural,
political and community groups to illustrate the versa-
tility of video in approaching diverse situations of
everyday life, whether from the viewpoint of "cultural
animation, " sociological research, or a surrealistic
game. Index and bibliography.

12. CRITICISM

A. TELEVISION

See also nos. 133, 210, 239.

277 Adler, Richard P. , editor. All in the Family--A Critical Appraisal. New York: Praeger Special Studies, Praeger Publishers, 1979. 384 pp.

This book describes the series' origins, development, and history, and includes actual scripts from three episodes and a sample of the program's initial reviews. Additional chapters analyze the show in terms of a larger context, and include discussions by social scientists determining the program's impact on viewers. Photographs, bibliography, and appendix.

278 Freeman, Don. In a Flea's Navel: A Critic's Love Affair with Television. San Diego, Calif.: A. S. Barnes, 1980. 229 pp.

Freeman is a syndicated TV critic. These amusing essays are about programs and the promise of television.

279 Himmelstein, Harold. On the Small Screen: New Directions in Television and Video Criticism. New York: Praeger Publishers, 1981. 180 pp.

A small group of writers are currently exploring video in the first steps toward formulating a video aesthetic, especially as it relates to traditional broadcast television. The author interviewed these writers about their work and their perception of its impact on both network television and the new video art form. Bibliography and index.

280 Mankiewicz, Frank. Remote Control: Television and
     the Manipulation of American Life. New York: Time
     Books, 1978. 308 pp.

         This book discusses the impact of television on
     our institution and our lives. It also describes the
     learning and social adaptation process with which tele-
     vision overwhelms the children in its audience. Very
     thorough and critical look at television.

281 Newcomb, Horace, editor. Television: The Critical
     View. 2nd edition. New York: Oxford University
     Press, 1979. 557 pp.

         A collection of essays dealing with television criti-
     cism. The first section deals with specific program
     types. The second section is comprised of essays
     that attempt to go beyond the specific meanings of
     specific programs or program types. The final sec-
     tion is concerned with what television is, how it is
     like and how it is different from other media.

282 Saldich, Anne Rawley. Electronic Democracy. New
     York: Praeger Publishers, 1979. 122 pp.

         Insightful analysis of television's impact on politics
     and government in the United States. The author sug-
     gests ways in which television media reality directly
     affects the quality of democracy in America. Index
     and bibliography.

283 Sass, Lauren, editor. Television: The American Medi-
     um in Crisis. New York: Facts on File, Inc., 1979.
     232 pp.

         Entire book consists of newspaper clippings which
     deal with various aspects of television broadcasting--
     mostly critical. Index.

284 White, Ned. Inside Television: A Guide to Critical
     Viewing. Palo Alto, Calif.: Science and Behavior,
     Books, Inc., n.d. 161 pp.

         This book makes no attempt to distinguish between
     good and bad programs, instead it is a democratic
     and even-handed try at explaining what makes almost
     any program work--or not work.

285 Winn, Marie. The Plug-in Drug: Television, Children and the Family. New York: Viking Press, 1977. 231 pp.

Based on interviews with hundreds of families, teachers and child specialists, this book presents a frightening picture of a society dominated by television; of children with poor verbal skills, an inability to concentrate, and a disinclination to read; of parents who are "hooked" on using television as a sedative for their preschool children. Some answers are provided, examples of how some families have found ways to control television successfully and how others have "unplugged" entirely and found new satisfactions in family life.

B. GENERAL

286 Rubin, Bernard, editor. Questioning Media Ethics. New York: Praeger Publishers, 1978. 320 pp.

Critics of the media who are practitioners as well criticize and clarify specific issues and real world situations representative of the ethical problems facing media practitioners today. Bibliography and filmography.

287 Winick, Charles, editor. Deviance and Mass Media. Volume 2, Beverly Hills, Calif.: Sage Publications, 1978. 312 pp.

This second volume of the Sage Reviews of Studies in Deviance focuses on deviance and mass media. A distinguished group of interdisciplinary scholars, communications experts, sociologists, educators, and journalists cover a wide range of topics on the attitude of the media toward various forms of deviant behavior.

13. PUBLIC BROADCASTING

A. PUBLIC RADIO

288 Brant, Billy G. College Radio Handbook. Blue Ridge
Summit, Pa.: TAB Books, 1979. 210 pp.

An examination of college radio stations: how
they are run, who runs them, and who pays for them.
The author explores commercial versus non-commer-
cial operations from a manager's point of view.
There is also a look at the future of college radio.
Appendix, illustrations, and index.

289 Jamison, Dean T., and Emile G. McAnany. Radio for
Education and Development. Beverly Hills, Calif.:
Sage Publications, Inc., 1978. 224 pp.

Radio's role as a delivery system for formal education is explored noting that in a world of rapidly
increasing television communication, radio remains
the dominant communication medium in developing
countries. References, bibliography, and appendix.

290 Public Radio and State Government. 2 volumes. Washington, D. C.: Public Telecommunications Press,
1981. Vol. I: 132 pp; Vol. II: 328 pp.

The first volume, "Description and Analysis" contains detailed state-by-state discussions on the funding
of public radio stations in that state, functions of various state agencies, funding levels, state level studies,
and associations. The second volume of the set provides facsimile reprints of state statutes dealing with
public broadcasting.

B. PUBLIC TELEVISION

291 Carnegie Commission on the Future of Public Broad-

casting. A Public Trust. New York: Bantam Books,
1979. 401 pp.

This report designs a new structure for public
television around four areas: programming, public
participation, financing, and technology dissemination. There is also a summary of findings and recommendations. Appendixes.

292 Ettema, James S. Working Together: A Study of Cooperation Among Producers, Educators and Researchers to Create Educational Television. Ann Arbor,
Mich.: Center for Research on Utilization of Scientific Knowledge, Institute for Social Research, University of Michigan, 1980. 212 pp.

Organizational power and politics are key issues
in this study, which concentrates on the management
and decision making aspects of the cooperative project.

293 Mahoney, Sheila; Nick Demartino; and Robert Stengel.
Keeping PACE with the New Television: Public Television and Changing Technology. New York: Carnegie Corporation of New York, VNU Books International, 1980. 281 pp.

PACE is a proposed new national pay cable network for performing arts, culture, and entertainment.
This study includes the proposal for PACE and reports on the industries which will affect the success
of the new network.

294 Wood, Donald N., and Donald G. Wylie. Educational
Telecommunications. Belmont, Calif.: Wadsworth
Publishing Company, 1977. 370 pp.

A comprehensive text dealing with both public
broadcasting and formal instructional television. Part
One discusses the foundation and historical background
of both public broadcasting and ITV. Part Two examines public broadcasting. Part Three stresses instructional design and Part Four is concerned with
the practical aspects of educational telecommunications
and outlines some basic considerations for production, distribution, utilization and research. Appendix
and index.

C. INSTRUCTIONAL TELEVISION

295 Botein, Michael. Videotape in Legal Education: A
      Study of Its Implications and a Manual for Its Use.
      New York: New York Law School, 1979.   70 pp.

      Reports the results of an American Bar Associa-
      tion study of the ways in which law teachers use
      videotape. It begins with an analysis of the possible
      uses of videotape in legal education, and then dis-
      cusses the results of a survey of 205 law teachers
      who used videotape as a teaching tool. It also dis-
      cusses the practical, institutional considerations in
      using videotape. Index and tables.

296 Kaplan, Don. Video in the Classroom: A Guide to
      Using Interactive Television.   White Plains, N. Y. :
      Knowledge Industry Publications, 1980.   160 pp.

      This book was designed to help teachers initiate
      "pupil-oriented" television in the schools.   Consider-
      ing the hodge-podge of topics I would recommend
      teachers to other, more organized production books.
      Topics range from values and religion, playing games
      with video, visual video techniques to manipulate the
      news.   That's quite a range for this brief book.   Bib-
      liography and index.

297 Lesser, Harvey. Television and the Preschool Child:
      A Psychological Theory of Instruction and Curriculum
      Development. New York: Academic Press, 1977.
      261 pp.

      This book includes chapters on an overview of
      young children as part of the television audience, the
      limits of instructional TV for young children, a re-
      assessment of Sesame Street, fostering reasoning abi-
      lities in young children, image and reality and a final
      chapter devoted to a proposal on effective ITV for the
      preschool child.

298 Schramm, Wilbur; Lyle M. Nelson; and Mere T. Betham.
      Bold Experiment: The Story of Educational Televi-
      sion in American Samoa.   Stanford, Calif. : Stanford
      University Press, 1981.   244 pp.

      The authors present the results of a 15-year study

following the introduction of television into American Samoa in 1964. Changes in academic achievement, leisure activity, attitudes, and values are all scrutinized. Both negative and positive effects of television were detected.

D. GENERAL

See also nos. 17, 18, 33.

299 Blakely, Robert J. To Serve the Public Interest: Educational Broadcasting in the United States. New York: Syracuse University Press, 1979. 274 pp.

A comprehensive account of the origins, philosophy, technologies, funding and persistence that sustained educational broadcasting from its beginning to today's sophisticated communications systems. Recommended for anyone interested in educational broadcasting. Index.

300 Gibson, George H. Public Broadcasting: The Role of the Federal Government, 1912-1976. New York: Praeger Special Studies, 1977. 256 pp.

Reviews all aspects of federal action on public broadcasting from legislative and executive efforts to cabinet and regulatory agency endeavors to formulate broadcasting policy and guidelines.

301 Jamison, Dean T.: Steven J. Klees; and Stuart J. Wells. The Cost of Educational Media: Guidelines for Planning and Evaluation. Volume 3. Beverly Hills, Calif.: Sage Publications, 1978. 256 pp.

In a book which pragmatically links budget and educational planning, the authors propose a methodology for the cost evaluation of both ongoing educational projects and projects which may be only in the planning stages. This study provides the methodology and case study supports that educators and administrators need to effectively consider those choices. The study is international in scope. Appendix and references.

302 Media Studies in Education. Reports and Papers on Mass Communication. No. 80. New York: UNIPUB, 1977. 92 pp.

This report is presented as a series of case studies, describing work in a number of countries where media education is an active force. Media education in Western Europe, Scandinavia, The USSR, and the USA are discussed. Bibliography.

303 Myrick, Howard A. , and Carol Keegan. Review of 1980 CPB Communication Research Findings. Washington, D. C. : Corporation for Public Broadcasting, 1981. 123 pp.

Consists of the highlights of the Office of Communication Research 1980 activities in research in each of the following areas: programming and audience trends; minority and special interest audience; formative and diagnostic research local station support; and development of improved methodologies for measuring audience interests and needs. Annotated bibliography, tables, and figures.

304 Sprague, Michael J. New Communications Media and Public Broadcasting: Impacts and Opportunities. New York: New York Law School, Communications Media Center, 1980. 29 pp.

A look at the economic, regulatory and legal aspects of interaction between the new technologies and PTV. Technologies discussed are cable TV, Subscription TV (STV), Multipoint Distribution Service (MDS), Direct Broadcast Satellites (DBS), Video-cassettes (VCR) and videodiscs (VDC).

14. AUDIENCE

A. TELEVISION

See also nos. 123, 127, 137, 142, 239, 242, 244, 245, 250, 280, 284, 285.

305 Baggaley, J. P. , and Steven Duck. The Dynamics of
     Television. Lexington, Mass. : Lexington Books,
     1977. 180 pp.

     The book extends the coverage provided by existing
     communication studies by examining the wider influ-
     ences of TV on the viewer. It gives more insight
     into the psychological impact of media in general.
     Index, graphs, and tables.

306 Baggaley, J. P. , and Margaret Ferguson. Television
     Techniques and Audience Reaction. New York: Prae-
     ger Publishers, 1980. 160 pp.

     Looking at the often unsuspected consequences of
     the methods employed by one of today's most influ-
     ential mediums, the authors discuss such aspects of
     television as the medium and its message; informa-
     tion and inference; performance variables; predicta-
     bility of media effects; and perspectives in television
     research.

307 Baran, Stanley J. The Viewer's Television Book: A
     Personal Guide to Understanding Television and Its
     Difference. Cleveland Heights, Ohio: Penrith Pub-
     lishing Company, 1980. 109 pp.

     This text tackles such issues as how and when TV
     effects may occur, TV violence, TV and children, TV
     and the family, and many other contemporary effects
     issues, all from the readers' perspective. Written

for the lay person or introductory student. The approach is unique as one can see by the chapter titles; for instance, chapter four is titled, How Come Farrah and Fonzie Never Get Zits?

308 Davis, Richard H. Television and the Aging Audience. Los Angeles: University of Southern California Press, 1980. 110 pp.

Included are chapters on the world of the old, the world of television, TV and the aging audience, program issues, using television, etc.

309 Fiske, John, and John Hartley. Reading Television. London: Methuen and Company, 1978. 223 pp.

Discusses television and reality or as the author puts it, "television mediates reality." Chapters cover the audiences, signs and codes on television, content analysis, etc. Since the book was written in Great Britain, it deals mostly with BBC programming although the authors appear to be discussing the topic on a universal level. Bibliography, index, and tables.

310 Frank, Ronald E., and Marshall G. Greenberg. The Public's Use of Television. Beverly Hills, Calif.: Sage Publications, Inc., 1980. 240 pp.

The authors conducted over 2,400 personal interviews throughout the United States, breaking the TV viewers' interests into 18 categories covering over 130 special interest areas ranging from sports to religion. These special interest areas were then matched to the personal needs they represent, resulting in a set of descriptions of TV audiences that reveals for the first time some of the reasons people use TV and how it fits into their lives.

311 Primeau, Ronald. The Rhetoric of Television. New York: Longman, Inc., 1978. 288 pp.

This book teaches readers how to understand, analyze, and enjoy the electronic media. The tools provided are based on classical rhetoric and include practical ways to identify how TV shows are created, structured and delivered in the unique form of the TV medium. Features include worksheets that involve readers in their own TV viewing, in-depth study of a variety of TV shows, classical rhetoric presented in plain English, and a review of the controversy over the effects of TV watching. Appendix, bibliography, glossary, and index.

15. RESEARCH

A. TELEVISION

See also nos. 24, 209, 242, 251.

312 Higgens, Patricia, and Marla Ray. Television's Action Arsenal: Weapon Use in Prime Time. Washington, D. C.: U. S. Conference of Mayors, 1978. 57 pp.

A study conducted to "fill a basic information gap in the television violence research literature, namely a lack of information on the instruments of violence." Appendixes.

313 Miller, Gerald R., and Norman E. Fontes. Videotape on Trial: A View from the Jury Box. Beverly Hills, Calif.: Sage Publishing Company, 1979. 224 pp.

The authors consider the effects on jurors when the traditional "live" courtroom environment is replaced by videotaped trials or testimony. Drawing upon their four years of research, as well as previous studies of juries, the authors seek to define some of the changes electronic technology imposes within the courtroom.

314 Murray, John P. Television and Youth: 25 Years of Research and Controversy. Boys Town, Neb.: The Boys Town Center for the Study of Youth Development, 1980. 278 pp.

This work is primarily bibliographic. Research is described and cited in narrative form and extensive bibliographies are provided. The citations are indexed by broad topic and recent work is listed separately as well. Index and bibliography.

315 Singer, Dorothy G.; Jerome L. Singer; and Diana M.
      Zuckerman. Teaching Television: How to Use TV
      to Your Children's Advantage. New York: The Dial
      Press, 1981. 210 pp.

      The authors answer questions parents ask and re-
      port in simple terms on major research.

B. GENERAL

316 Dordick, Herbert S., editor. Proceedings of the Sixth
      Annual Telecommunications Policy Research Confer-
      ence. Lexington, Mass.: Lexington Books, 1979.
      475 pp.

      A comprehensive summary of latest developments
      in telecommunications research. This book explores
      such issues as television and social reality, alterna-
      tive broadcast and non-broadcast technologies, net-
      work technology, services, etc. Notes, figures,
      tables, and references.

317 Eiselein, E. B. Broadcast Communications Research
      Materials. Tucson, Ariz.: Authors Services, 1981.

      This is a "general introduction to the major ap-
      plications of social science research methods in broad-
      casting and related industries." Chapters deal with
      background for understanding broadcast communica-
      tions research, use of communications research in
      broadcasting, survey research, reading the ratings
      books for radio and television and more.

318 Fletcher, James E., editor. Handbook of Radio and
      TV Broadcasting: Research Procedures in Audience,
      Program and Revenues. New York: Van Nostrand
      Reinhold, 1981. 336 pp.

      Eleven chapters covering reading the market re-
      port, telephone surveys, sampling, interviewing, as-
      certainment research, message and program testing,
      etc. There are many examples of research reports.
      Appendix and index.

319 Hirsh, Paul M.; Peter V. Miller; and F. Gerald Kline.
      Strategies for Communication Research. Beverly
      Hills, Calif.: Sage Publications, 1977. 288 pp.

The editors of this annual have targeted three important topics in communications research for consideration. They have gathered here some of the most scholarly and thought provoking research on organizational analysis and field study quantitative data collection and modeling, and conceptualization of time and temporal order.

320   "Media, Culture and Society," International Journal (quarterly). New York: Academic Press.

Provides an international forum for the presentation of research and discussion of media within their political, cultural, and historical context.

321   Tan, Alexis S. Mass Communication Theories and Research. Columbus, Ohio: Grid Publishing Company, 1981. 311 pp.

A basic text for mass communications theory. Meets the need for an up-to-date, in-depth, research oriented discussion of mass communications theories. Index and figures.

16. BROADCASTING CAREERS

A. RADIO

322 Ramsey, Dan. How to Be a Disc Jockey. Blue Ridge
     Summit, Pa.: TAB Books, 1981. 224 pp.

       Tells how to break into and succeed in radio.

B. GENERAL

323 Allosso, Michael. Your Career in Theatre, Radio, Tele-
     vision or Filmmaking. New York: Arco Publishing
     Company, 1978. 191 pp.

       The book was written for high school students who
     may wish to prepare for a career in one of the areas
     mentioned in the title. Each chapter includes advice
     from working professionals, answers to frequently
     asked questions and information on qualifications,
     duties and responsibilities. Appendix, glossary, pho-
     tographs, illustrations, and diagrams.

324 Gross, Lynne Schaffer. The Internship Experience.
     Belmont, Calif.: Wadsworth Publishing Company,
     1981. 124 pp.

       Practical guide to general procedures and practices
     of student internship. The orientation of the book is
     toward communication internships; that is, radio and
     television, film, advertising, and journalism. A much
     needed book that has finally arrived.

17. INTERNATIONAL

A. EUROPE

325 Balfour, Michael. Propaganda in War 1939-1945: Organizations, Policies and Publics in Britain and Germany. Boston: Routledge and Kegan Paul, 1979. 520 pp.

This book deals with both British and German propaganda during the Second World War, including what was said at home and what was said abroad to the enemy. It also gives a detailed analysis of the way the war news was handled on both sides. It gives, too, a new view of the nature and effects of propaganda and how publicity should be fitted into the machinery of government. Index.

326 Briggs, Asa. History of Broadcasting in the United Kingdom. Volume IV. Sound and Vision. New York: Oxford University Press, 1979. 1096 pp.

Covers the ten years following World War II. Each volume is complete within itself. Bibliography and index.

327 Brown, Ray. Characteristics of Local Media Audiences. England: Saxon House; distributed by Renouf USA, Inc.: Brookfield, Vt., 1978. 130 pp.

This book reports the first detailed investigation of the satisfactions both listeners and readers find in their local media. It describes the "uses and qualifications" approach to the study of communications and explains how this approach is applied in the field. The book deals with the British audience. Index, bibliography, and tables.

328   Comstock, George; Steven Chaffee; Nathan Katzman;
       Maxwell McCombs; and Donald Roberts. Television
       and Human Behavior. New York: Columbia Univer-
       sity Press, 1979. 581 pp.

       The authors have attempted to cover the entire rele-
       vant scientific literature on television in English, ex-
       amining more than 2500 books, articles, reports, and
       documents. The material is grouped under the fol-
       lowing headings: Overview, What's On, The Audience,
       Living with Television, One Highly Attracted Public
       (children), Four Highly Attracted Publics (women,
       blacks, the poor, and the elderly), Politics and Pur-
       chases, the Psychology of Behavioral Effects, and the
       Future. Index and references.

329   Crane, Rhonda J. The Politics of International Standards:
       France and the Color TV War. Norwood, N. J. :
       Ablex Publishing Company, 1979. 165 pp.

       Examines the adoption of color TV standards in
       France, including the politics, technology, interna-
       tional trade relations, and bargaining involved in
       standard setting, showing the degree to which techni-
       cal standards are the result of political and economic
       factors. Appendixes, bibliography, and index.

330   Fisher, Desmond. Broadcasting in Ireland. Boston:
       Routledge and Kegan Paul, 1978. 120 pp.

       The author outlines in a highly readable fashion
       the historical and sociological background of the Ire-
       land of today and chronicles the progress of its broad-
       casting services in the context of its post independ-
       ence development. Bibliography, appendix, and tables.

331   Glasgow University Media Group. Bad News. London:
       Routledge and Kegan Paul, 1976. 310 pp.

       The authors describe how they monitored all tele-
       vision news dealing with economic affairs in Great
       Britain for a six-month period. The general contours
       of industrial news coverage are examined and the spe-
       cial relationship between trade unions and media are
       discussed. The results of their research gives a new
       insight into the picture of industrial society that TV
       news constructs, at least in Great Britain. Index,
       appendix, tables, and figures.

332   Glasgow University Media Group.   More Bad News.
      London: Routledge and Kegan Paul, 1980.   483 pp.

            A follow-up to the first edition, Bad News listed
      above.   This column is divided into three parts: the
      first is a case study of the reporting of an economic
      crisis and claims that there is bias in the way in-
      dustrial disputes are covered; the second part deals
      with language, linguistics and their social and politi-
      cal implications; the third section is an ambitious
      attempt to use print media to somehow capture an
      electronic medium.   Provides a good look at tele-
      vision news.

333   Haak, Kees van der.   Broadcasting in the Netherlands.
      London: Routledge and Kegan Paul, 1977.   93 pp.

            This book analyzes Dutch broadcasting.   It de-
      scribes the historical traditions of Dutch Society, re-
      counts the ways in which radio and later TV were
      set up, and shows how recent changes in Dutch poli-
      tics, culture and economy, and technological innova-
      tion posed a new set of challenges.   Bibliography,
      appendix, and tables.

334   Mickiewicz, Ellen Propper.   Media and the Russian
      Public.   New York: Praeger Publishers, 1981.   176
      pp.

            This is the first major study of media and the
      Russian public based on Soviet sources.   The author
      has gone through a vast number of Soviet journals to
      report the results of every major study done on the
      Russians and their opinions and behavior in regard
      to television, newspapers, films, theater, and music.

335   Munro, Colin R.   Television Censorship and the Law.
      England: Saxon House; distributed by Renouf USA,
      Inc. , Brookfield, Vermont, 1979.   194 pp.

            One of the few books that systematically and cri-
      tically surveys the limits of freedom to televise.
      The book deals with television broadcasting in England.
      Index, table of cases, bibliography, table of statutes,
      and notes.

336   Paulu, Burton.   Television and Radio in the United King-

dom. Minneapolis, Minn.: University of Minnesota Press, 1981. 476 pp.

This book examines British broadcasting's local structure, financial basis, personnel policies, and technical facilities with reference to its program services. The author describes both domestic and overseas programs and he reviews the findings of audience research. His detached approach as a foreign observer enhances the value of the book and through it he freely expresses his own views. He is careful to maintain distinctions between fact and appraisal. Index.

337 Report of the Committee on the Future of Broadcasting. London: Her Majesty's Stationery Office, 1977. 522 pp.

Although the Committee's immediate concern was the special situation of British broadcasting in the seventies, it was, in fact, responding to the common underlying dilemmas of Western-style broadcasting systems throughout the world. The committee studied various aspects of broadcasting in a dozen foreign countries as background to its deliberations. American readers will recognize in the report all of the familiar broadcasting concerns, such as access, fairness, renewal standards, children's advertising, sex and violence, monopoly, media cross ownership, consumer intervention, and so on.

338 Seglow, Peter. Trade Unionism in Television. England: Saxon House; distributed by Renouf USA, Inc., Brookfield, Vermont, 1978. 287 pp.

In this book the author looks at the pattern of militancy which has characterized trade unionism in British TV and contrasts it to relative tranquility that, until recently, was found in BBC television. Index, notes, and tables.

339 Smith, Anthony, editor. Television and Political Life. New York: St. Martin's Press, Inc., 1979. 261 pp.

This book takes six countries (Britain, France, Germany, Italy, Holland and Sweden) and examines

the ways in which governments and legislatures have
either come to terms with or continue to threaten
the independence of political broadcasters. Each con-
tributor is a media expert, either a citizen of the
country concerned or a veteran foreign observer and
each tries to access the ways in which the society's
political culture has been affected by the medium of
television.

340 Thomas, Ruth. Broadcasting and Democracy in France.
     Philadelphia: Temple University Press, 1976. 211
     pp.

     Examines the history, structure, and economics
     of French broadcasting from 1945. Discusses the
     relationship between broadcasting and government.
     Analyzes the two central features of a democratic
     broadcasting system. Bibliography, index, and ap-
     pendix.

341 Tracey, Michael. The Production of Political Television.
     London: Routledge and Kegan Paul, Ltd. , 1978. 282
     pp.

     The purpose of this book is to consider the ways
     in which political television programs are shaped and
     formed within the multitude of contexts and conditions
     which prevail at any one moment. Political program-
     ming is defined here as programs dealing with the
     policy-making process within Britain. Bibliography,
     and index.

342 Williams, Arthur. Broadcasting and Democracy in West
     Germany. Philadelphia: Temple University Press,
     1976. 198 pp.

     Traces the development of the German broadcasting
     system from 1945 as its democratic foundations evol-
     ved. Bibliography, index, and tables.

B. ASIA

343 Adhikarya, Ronny. Broadcasting in Peninsular Malaysia.
     Boston: Routledge and Kegan Paul, 1977. 102 pp.

     A brief description of Malaysia's social, economic,

and political situation are given followed by an ex-
ploration of the difficulties facing authorities who have
to cope with racial and political tensions within the
community. The study is wide in scope and includes
the government controlled radio/TV, the Royal Aus-
tralian Air Force Radio, magazines, telecommunications and newspapers. The structure of broadcasting
now is explored and the future trends are discussed.
Bibliography, appendix, figures, and tables.

344 Bae-ho, Hahn. Communication Policies in the Republic
     of Korea. New York: UNIPUB, 1978. 50 pp.

     One of a series of monographs dealing with the
     communication policies in various Asian countries.
     Includes mass media structure, the government and
     mass media and the role of mass media. Tables and
     appendix.

345 Kato, Hidetoshi. Communication Policies in Japan. New
     York: UNIPUB, 1978. 57 pp.

     Another in a series of monographs on communica-
     tion policies done for UNESCO. Others in the series
     include Europe and South America. Contents are
     similar to the study reported elsewhere in this text
     on Korea. Tables and appendix.

346 Lent, John A. , editor. Broadcasting in Asia and the
     Pacific. Philadelphia: Temple University Press,
     1978. 429 pp.

     Anthology covering the instructional and functional
     foundations of broadcasting in forty-four countries,
     territories, and dependencies, ranging from West Asia
     to the South Pacific Islands. Contributors include in-
     ternational communication scholars, trainers, and
     practitioners. Topics covered include historical de-
     velopment, control, ownership programming, facili-
     ties, financing and advertising, audiences, training
     and research. Bibliography, index, and tables.

347 Lerner, Daniel, editor. Asian Communications: Re-
     search, Training, Planning. Honolulu: East West
     Center Communications Institute, 1977. 138 pp.

     Consists mainly of eight papers on using commer-

cial resources for audience research, a content analysis model of the press, provincial press and national
development, a comparative analysis of mass communications systems, building the Asian Communications
network, and more. Tables.

348 Lyons, Nick. The Sony Vision. New York: Crown,
     1976. 235 pp.

     Almost a pictorial history of the development of
     The Sony Corporation. Takes the reader from Sony's
     beginnings as Tokyo Telecommunications Laboratory
     to the Betamax CRA. Good look at the development
     of a company that has had such an impact on the
     video field. Bibliography, index, illustrations, and
     photographs.

C.   LATIN AMERICA

349 Mayo, John K.; Robert C. Hornik; and Emile G. Mc-
     Anany. Educational Reform with Television: The
     El Salvador Experience. Stanford, Calif.: Stanford
     University Press, 1976. 216 pp.

     This is a detailed report of the planning, develop-
     ment, operations, results and problems of a unique
     experiment in instructional television. It deals with
     an experiment conducted in El Salvador which proved
     to be such a success that the authors conclude that
     it could be a model for other developing countries.
     Index, appendix, tables, and photographs.

350 Sanders, Ron. Broadcasting in Guyana. Boston: Rout-
     ledge and Kegan Paul, 1978. 77 pp.

     This book explores the acute problems the country
     faces in its struggle to develop a broadcasting system
     designed to serve the interests of the community as
     a whole. Bibliography, appendix, and maps.

D.   CANADA

351 Allard, T. J. Straight Up: Private Broadcasting in
     Canada: 1918-1958. Ottawa, Ontario: Canadian
     Communications Foundation, 1979. 280 pp.

Bluntly challenges nearly every generally accepted concept about Canadian broadcasting. Describes the development of broadcasting from the day of the crystal set right through to color television. It outlines public and behind the scenes events involved in the struggle to shape the structure of Canada's broadcasting and who should control it. Bibliography.

352 Hallman, Eugene S. Broadcasting in Canada. Boston: Routledge and Kegan Paul, 1977. 90 pp.

Provides an account of the evolution, present structure, and future possibilities of Canada's unique broadcasting system. Using up-to-date, inside information, it shows how conditions and pressures have led Canadians to construct a single system of broadcasting regulated by an independent public authority. Appendix and tables.   226305

353 Peers, Frank W. The Public Eye: Television and Politics of Canadian Broadcasting, 1952-1968. Toronto: University of Toronto Press, 1979. 459 pp.

Traces the beginnings and development of TV from 1952 to the passing of the Broadcast Act in 1968, focusing on decisions made by governments on broadcasting activities. Index.

E. PROPAGANDA

354 Bogart, Leo. Premises for Propaganda: The United States Information Agency's Operating Assumptions in the Cold War. New York: Free Press, 1976. 250 pp.

The study reported in this book was commissioned in 1953 by the U. S. Information Agency to help plan its own program of research. For years it remained classified as "confidential" and remained locked up. Its release came about after the passage of the Federal Freedom of Information Act. It was published because of its historical and political research and due to its intimate picture of how a propaganda organization operates. Topics covered include truth and credibility, protecting America, using the media, etc. Index and appendix.

F. GENERAL

355 Cherry, Colin. World Communication: Threat or Prom-
     ise? Revised edition. New York: John Wiley and
     Sons, 1978. 229 pp.

     This book attacks many popular beliefs about com-
     munication and examines the influence of technologi-
     cal developments upon international relations. It ex-
     amines the nature of human communication, regarding
     it as a sharing process and it considers the constraints
     of various technological systems. The book also of-
     fers graphical and statistical evidence, leading to the
     conclusion that international communication encourages
     the growth of multiple federations rather than centra-
     lization of power. Index, bibliography, and figures.

356 Contreras, Eduardo. Cross-Cultural Broadcasting. New
     York: UNIPUB, 1976. 49 pp.

     Some of the topics covered in this report are use
     of satellite broadcasting to achieve a wide diffusion
     of television programming of multicultural audiences;
     international program sales which insure that pro-
     grams are suitable for the cultures which they reach;
     regional communications systems; and cooperation in
     program production. Bibliography.

357 Fascell, Dante B. , editor. International News: Free-
     dom Under Attack. Beverly Hills, Calif. : Sage Pub-
     lications, 1979. 320 pp.

     The articles contained in this book are products
     of the Georgetown University Center for strategic and
     International Studies Program in international com-
     munications. Topics cover international broadcasting;
     mass media and the Third World; international news
     and the American media; and access denied: the poli-
     tics of press censorship. References.

358 Gerbner, George, editor. Mass Media Policies in Chang-
     ing Cultures. New York: John Wiley and Son, 1977.
     291 pp.

     Examines international trends, new directions, and
     theoretical developments in mass media policies around
     the world. Part I is a survey of international trends,

with various articles describing early Western leader-
ship and recent shifts in the balance of power.   Part
II explores new directions in communications policy
in traditional, transitional and revolutionary societies.
Part III presents developments in theory and research
that can be useful in considering different approaches
to crosscultural comparative media studies.   Index.

359   Homet, Roland S., Jr.   Politics, Cultures and Com-
       munications: American Approaches to Communica-
       tions Policymaking.   New York: Praeger Publishers,
       1979.   126 pp.

       This companion volume to Communications for
       Tomorrow, is a concise analysis of similarities and
       differences existing in the communications policies
       of France, Great Britain, West Germany, Italy, Swe-
       den, and the Netherlands on one hand, and Canada
       and the United States on the other.   The author makes
       comparisons between elitist European broadcasting
       and its populist oriented North American counterpart.

360   Katz, Elihu, and George Wendall.   Broadcasting in the
       Third World.   Cambridge, Mass.: Harvard Univer-
       sity Press, 1977.   305 pp.

       This book offers complete coverage of the prob-
       lems and promises of broadcasting in the Third World.
       The information in the book would be of interest to
       sociologists, political scientists, and communication
       specialists.   The book is based on field research
       conducted in eleven developing countries.   It is divided
       into four parts: Promise, Process, Performance, and
       Prospect.   The authors conclude with a series of
       recommendations which challenge most of the assump-
       tions upon which the principles and practices of broad-
       casting are based.   Index, appendix, and tables.

361   McCavitt, William E., editor.   Broadcasting Around the
       World.   Blue Ridge Summit, Pa.: TAB Books, 1981.
       336 pp.

       Covers broadcasting in eighteen countries from
       various parts of the globe.   Contributors range from
       professionals in the field to professors in universi-
       ties where broadcast communication is taught.   Writ-
       ing styles are as different as the contributing coun-

tries. Basically, the content covers the history,
present, and the future of broadcasting in each country included. Index, photographs, bibliography, and
tables.

362 The New World Information Order: Issues in the World
     Administrative Radio Conference and Transborder
     Data Flow. New York: Communications Media Cen-
     ter, New York Law School, 1979. 40 pp.

     This collection of essays discusses two of the most
     pressing issues in international communications--possible
     effects of the 1979 World Administrative Radio Confer-
     ence (WARC) and the restrictions on transfer of com-
     puter data from one nation to another. Index.

363 Nordenstreng, Kaarle, and Herbert I. Schiller. National
     Sovereignty and International Communication. Nor-
     wood, N. J. : Ablex Publishing Corporation, 1979.
     304 pp.

     Sixteen worldwide experts examine the new and
     explosive problems in the traffic rules of interna-
     tional communications from the perspective of the
     social sciences, law, journalism, international poli-
     tics, even technology--all from a pluralistic, largely
     non-Western point of view. It challenges conventional
     thinking on such concepts as the free flow of infor-
     mation, cultural integrity, the role of communica-
     tions in national development, the right of nations to
     control their own cultural/communication space, and
     more, including satellite broadcasting.

364 Read, William H. America's Mass Media Merchants.
     Baltimore: Johns Hopkins University Press, 1976.
     209 pp.

     An analysis of the extent and impact of foreign
     dissemination of the product of American television,
     film, and print media.

365 Teheranian, Majid; Farhad Hakinzadeh; and Marcello L.
     Vidale, editors. Communications Policy for National
     Development: A Comparative Perspective. London
     and Boston: Routledge and Kegan Paul, 1977. 286
     pp.

Covering a wide international field and with the emphasis on communications in developing countries, this book is a good reference work for institutions concerned with communications as well as for students of the media. Subjects covered include policy, governance and planning in the field of mass communications. Tables.

366 Wallestein, G. D. International Telecommunication Agreements. Volume II. Dobbs Ferry, N. Y. : Oceana Publications, 1980.

This series has two purposes: one is to put on record what the International Telecommunication Union has accomplished and the other is to show why and how the I. T. U. 's agreement-making system may serve as a general model. For the first purpose, the I. T. U. system is described and analyzed in Part I of the first volume. For the second purpose, the I. T. U. type system is subjected to a multidisciplinary inquiry. This inquiry is supported by specific I. T. U. actions and cases that are fully referenced in the documentary parts of the series. Index.

18.   TECHNICAL

A.   AUDIO

367   Orr, William I.   Radio Handbook.   21st edition.   Indianapolis, Ind.:   Howard W. Sams and Company,
1978.   1135 pp.

This new edition covers basic fundamentals plus
the latest electronic techniques and practices.   It up-
dates materials presented in earlier editions.   Technical book in all aspects.   Index, figures, photographs,
and glossary.

B.   VIDEO

368   Costigan, Daniel M.   Electronic Delivery of Documents
and Graphics.   New York: Van Nostrand Reinhold
Co., 1978.   344 pp.

Discusses facsimile communication development
and application today with details on how it works,
current equipment, etc.   Chapters deal with trans-
mission, quality of image, electronic standards, other
systems (including comment on the many new videotext approaches) and the outlook for further changes.

369   Ennes, Harold E.   Television Broadcasting: Equipment,
Systems and Operating Fundamentals.   2nd edition.
Indianapolis, Ind.:   Howard W. Sams & Company,
1979.   656 pp.

Covers the entire television broadcast system, a
valuable reference for the practicing technician.   Exercises at the end of each chapter.   Technical book.
Index, glossary, appendixes, figures, photographs,
and tables.

370 Ennes, Harold E.   Television Broadcasting: Tape Re-
     cording Systems.   2nd edition.   Indianapolis, Ind. :
     Howard W. Sams & Company, 1979.   528 pp.

         Provides basic knowledge of the primary functions
     of videotape equipment.   Coverage ranges from basic
     theory to testing and maintenance of complete sys-
     tems.   Technical book.   Index, appendix, tables,
     figures, and photographs.

371 Ingram, Dave.   The Complete Handbook of Slow-Scan
     TV.   Blue Ridge Summit, Pa. :   TAB Books, 1977.
     304 pp.

         Technical work which deals with setting up and
     operating a slow scan TV amateur station.   The book
     details the system, the various equipment needed,
     operating procedures, and satellite communications.
     Photographs, and diagrams.

372 Kybett, Harry.   Video Tape Recorders.   2nd edition.
     Indianapolis, Ind. :   Howard W. Sams & Company,
     1978.   400 pp.

         Revised and updated edition about helical VTRs.
     The fundamentals of videotape recording are described
     and the basic problems and their solutions are outlined.
     A short history of video recording is given plus nu-
     merous examples of electronic circuits and mechani-
     cal systems.   Good reference.   Index, figures, and
     photographs.

373 Park, Rolla Edward.   Projecting the Growth of Televi-
     sion Broadcasting: Implications for Spectrum Use.
     Santa Monica, Calif. :   Rand Corporation, 1976.   308
     pp.

         This study, prepared for the FCC, was to esti-
     mate the number of commercial UHF TV stations
     that are likely to come on the air between the pres-
     ent and 1990, and to determine whether spectrum re-
     sources already allocated will be adequate to meet
     this demand.   Appendixes.

374 Shiers, George.   Technical Development of Television.
     New York: Arno Press, 1977.

         This collection of thirty items surveys technical

progress from the early proposals of the late 1870's
to the inception of modern color TV.   There are orig-
nal papers by pioneers, contemporary articles, reports on individual and corporate activities, accounts
by historians and national committee records.   Illustrations and references.

C.   GENERAL

375   Broadcast and Communications.   New York: Arco Pub-
      lishing Company, 1978.   118 pp.

      Full of straightforward technical information.   There
      is also much to interest those less scientifically mind-
      ed, including the history of communications from sema-
      phore to space exploration.   Both television and ra-
      dio are discussed from their earliest days to the
      present.   Finally, the future and satellites which
      could link the world for multi-national broadcasting,
      lasers, and new technologies for transmission of data
      between space probes and earth are explored.

376   Cunningham, John E.   The Complete Broadcasting Anten-
      na Handbook: Design, Installation, Operation and
      Maintenance.   Blue Ridge Summit, Pa.:   TAB Books,
      1977.   450 pp.

      This book on antennas has all the knowledge needed
      to specify, design, operate, maintain, protect and
      perform required measurements on any (AM, FM, TV)
      antenna system.   Illustrations and index.

377   Martin, James.   Future Developments in Telecommuni-
      cations.   2nd edition.   Englewood Cliffs, N. J.:   Pren-
      tice-Hall, Inc., 1978.   668 pp.

      Text and diagrams by an IBM scientist look to the
      near and distant future of cable television and other
      means of transmission, tie-ins to computers, spec-
      trum use changes, satellites, mobile radio transre-
      ceivers, etc.

378   Muncheryan, Hrand.   Laser Technology.   2nd edition.
      Indianapolis, Ind.:   Howard W. Sams & Company,
      1979.   288 pp.

      Complete book on lasers and their application in a

variety of areas including communication, holography and television projection to name a few. Rather technical. Index, appendixes, photographs, illustrations, figures, and tables.

379 Veley, Victor, F. C. First Class Commercial FCC License Study Guide. Blue Ridge Summit, Pa.: TAB Books, 1978. 378 pp.

A quick prep course/review guide to vital broadcast electronics information to help obtain a first class FCC license. Each chapter contains problems and solutions plus practice problems. Illustrations.

19. CABLE TELEVISION

A. REGULATION

380 Biriny, Anne E. Chronology of State Cable Television
Regulation, 1947-1978. Cambridge, Mass.: Harvard
University, 1978. 20 pp.

An evaluation of cable TV regulation in the U. S.
presented by means of a chronological and contextual
matrix, giving decisions made by state legislatures,
state courts, and state regulatory agencies. Also included are decisions of the federal courts and the
FCC.

381 Jacobson, Robert E. Municipal Control of Cable Communications. New York: Praeger Special Studies,
1977. 152 pp.

Traces the recent historical development of cable
in an urban context; the role of telecommunications
as a public good; the failure of private entrepreneurs
to fill this role and the means for cities to use cable.
Concludes that cities should take the initiative in
developing cable systems and opposes private ownership. Summary, appendix, and bibliography.

382 Rivkin, Steven R. A New Guide to Federal Cable Television Regulations. Cambridge, Mass.: MIT Press,
1978. 336 pp.

A complete legal handbook for the cable TV industry. Contains current (1978) FCC regulations with
item by item, definitions and interpretations, all based
on actual court and administrative proceedings. Appendix.

B. PROGRAMMING

383   Berryman, Sue E.; Tora K. Bikson; and Judith S. Baze-
      more.   Cable, Two-Way Video and Educational Pro-
      gramming: The Case of Daycare.   Santa Monica,
      Calif.: Rand, 1978. 158 pp.

> This report on the two-way video experiment serves
> two purposes.   First, the report is written for citi-
> zens and public officials who are concerned about the
> quality of care in daycare facilities and who might
> wish to consider telecommunications as a means of
> in-service training for caregivers.   Second, it is a
> preliminary study of the value of two-way video.   It
> suggests how two-way video can be used to produce
> local program services.   Bibliography, illustrations,
> and tables.

C. PRODUCTION

384   Forbes, Dorothy, and Sanderson Layng.   The New Com-
      municators: A Guide to Community Programming.
      Washington, D. C.: Communications Press, 1978.
      117 pp.

> This book, although written for a Canadian audience,
> is a valuable guide for those involved in innovative
> uses of local channels on American cable television
> systems.   The book was written for the programming
> director and it offers a wealth of helpful ideas for
> his or her many roles as manager, program consul-
> tant, television advisor, and public relations officer.
> Bibliography.

385   Schiller, Don; Bill E. Brock; and Fred Rigby.
      CATV Program Origination and Production.   Blue
      Ridge Summit, Pa.: TAB Books, 1978. 252 pp.

> This book tells how to develop and schedule CATV
> shows, how to conduct market surveys, how to sell
> advertising time and how to use CATV equipment.   It
> is a readable, easily understood book which will serve
> as a good reference for those interested in CATV.   In-
> dex, appendixes, glossary, photographs, and charts.

386   Scott, James D.   Bringing Premium Entertainment into

the Home via Pay Cable TV.   Ann Arbor, Mich.:
University of Michigan, 1977.   60 pp.

This monograph reviews in detail the questions
that cable television operators should consider if they
are weighing the possibility of adding premium entertainment (pay-cable television) to their basic cable
service.   Covers a range of topics from hardware to
aesthetics.   Tables.

D.   TECHNICAL CATV

387   Rheinfelder, William A.   CATV System Engineering.
       Blue Ridge Summit, Pa.:   TAB Books, n.d.   294 pp.

       Practical advice and techniques on CATV design.
       Shows how to avoid all the most common design pit-
       falls.   Illustrations and glossary.

E.   GENERAL

See also nos. 7, 32, 92, 306, 316.

388   Botein, Michael, and Ben Paark, editors.   What to Do
       When Cable Comes to Town.   New York: New York
       Law School, 1980.   115 pp.

       This set of franchise and related documents pro-
       vides "state of the art" drafting of local cable tele-
       vision franchises.   These documents provide basic
       checklists and language for cable television franchising.
       Index.

389   Current Developments in CATV, 1981.   New York:
       Practicing Law Institute, 1981.   635 pp.

       Deals with First Amendment Issues, pole attach-
       ments, FCC regulations, program rights, copyright
       concerning broadcast signals, access channels, fran-
       chising and a summary of cable in 1981 as compared
       to 1980.   Charts.

390   Friedlander, Rena, and Michael Botein.   The Process
       of Cable Television Franchising: A New York City
       Case Study.   New York: New York Law School, 1980.
       110 pp.

A special report commissioned by New York City. It traces the development of New York City's procedures for franchising cable television systems from 1962 through 1980. The book not only analyzes this rather confusing history, but also highlights key points at which the franchising process either broke down or was deficient. Index.

391 Hollowell, Mary Louise, editor. The Cable/Broadband Communications Book: 1977-1978. Washington, D. C.: Communications Press, Inc., 1977. 230 pp.

Contains new information and some new subjects such as basic data on communications satellites, fiber optics and home video systems, as well as the role of broadband communications to rural areas. Glossary and tables.

392 Jaberg, Gene, and Louis G. Wargo, Jr. The Video Pencil: Cable Communications for Church and Community. Washington, D. C.: University of America, 1980. 156 pp.

An analysis of the ways in which mass communications have affected the Church in American society.

393 Park, Rolla Edward. Audience Diversion Due to Cable Television: A Statistical Analysis of Data. Santa Monica, Calif.: Rand, 1979. 59 pp.

This report was prepared for the Federal Communications Commission by Rand. This report provides some answers, based on a statistical analysis of new audience data assembled by the FCC's Cable Bureau. It is a companion report to Audience Diversion Due to Cable TV: Supporting Data. Tables.

394 Veith, Richard. Talk Back TV: Two Way Cable Television. Blue Ridge Summit, Pa.: TAB Books, 1976. 238 pp.

Discusses the concepts and capabilities of two-way cable television. Includes pay cable, prototypes, computers and projections for the future. Illustrations, selected bibliography, appendix, and index.

20. CORPORATE VIDEO

395 Black, Gilbert. Trends in Management Development and Education: An Economic Study. New York: Knowledge Industry, 1979. 198 pp.

This book covers the educational aspects of management development, its economic growth, its cost to organizations, and the educational methods it employs, the equipment and software it uses, and the consultants, universities and other outside institutions used by corporate management development departments in carrying out development programs. Tables, appendix, bibliography, and index.

396 Bland, Michael. The Executive's Guide to TV and Radio Appearances. White Plains, N.Y.: Knowledge Industries Publications, 1980. 138 pp.

This book is a guide to successful interviews on television. It not only briefs the reader for appearing on radio and TV, but also gives advice on how to make the optimum use of them for free publicity, especially local radio. A checklist appears at the end of most chapters with suggestions on what to do and say, attire, plus other basic information. Appendix and photographs.

397 Brush, Judith M., and Douglas P. Brush. Private Television Communications: Into the Eighties--The Third Brush Report. Berkeley Heights, N.J.: International Television Association, 1981. 204 pp.

Discusses the results of a survey the authors conducted concerning the use of private television today and attempts to forecast where it is heading. It also touches on the new technology such as video disc, VHS and Beta 1/2-inch formats, and the office of the future.

112

398   Bunyan, John A. , and James C. Crimmins.   Television
      and Management: The Manager's Guide to Video.
      New York: Knowledge Industry, 1977.   151 pp.

      Takes you behind the scenes in a fictional corpora-
      tion to illustrate how communication problems grow
      along with a business--how one corporation turned to
      television in a desperate hope that it would resolve
      these problems.   Index, graphs, and appendix.

399   Bunyan, John A. ; James C. Crimmins; and N. Kyri Wat-
      son.   Practical Video: The Managers Guide to Appli-
      cations.   New York: Knowledge Industries, 1978.
      201 pp.

      Case histories including business, government,
      education, and health uses of television for training
      purposes.   Good reference for managers of training
      centers utilizing video.   Index, selected bibliography,
      glossary, photographs, illustrations, and graphs.

400   Hilton, Jack, and Mary Knoblauch.   On Television: A
      Survival Guide for Media Interviews.   New York:
      Amacom, 1980.   185 pp.

      Interview techniques for the uninitiated are ex-
      plained by a management consultant.   It is aimed at
      business people in the position of spokesperson for a
      cause or a company.

401   McGuire, Jerry.   How to Write, Direct and Produce Ef-
      fective Business Films and Documentaries.   Blue
      Ridge Summit, Pa. :   TAB Books, 1978.   292 pp.

      An informative, behind-the-scenes look at how to
      research a presentation, generate a script outline,
      write an effective script, and produce a documentary.
      Also includes information on budgeting and has sample
      contracts, budgets, scripts, etc.   Illustrations, index,
      and appendixes.

402   Matrazzo, Donna.   The Corporate Scriptwriting Book.
      Philadelphia: Media Concepts Press, Inc. , 1980.
      197 pp.

      A practical step-by-step guide to writing scripts
      for organizations.   Offers an understanding of the

interaction among the writer, the client, the script,
the systems, and other employees.   Illustrations.

403   Nilles, Jack M.   The Telecommunications-Transportation
      Tradeoff: Options for Tomorrow.   New York: John
      Wiley and Sons, 1976.   196 pp.

      Discusses how top management, corporate and in-
      dustrial planners, heads of information processing
      and communications divisions can reduce the costs of
      operations.   Included are such subjects as telecom-
      munications, computers and transportation industries,
      interactive instructional television, telecommuting,
      and case studies.   Index, appendix, tables, and fig-
      ures.

404   Rubin, Bernard.   Big Business and the Mass Media.
      Lexington, Mass.:   D. C. Heath Company, 1977.
      208 pp.

      Analyzes the problems corporate executives and
      the press encounter as they interact in presenting
      news to the public.   The discussion includes an exam-
      ination of the specific situations faced by the media,
      by giant corporations, by public interest groups, and
      by alert citizens.   Tables.

405   Thompson, Tom.   Organizational TV News.   Philadel-
      phia: Media Concepts Press, 1980.   217 pp.

      Discusses why the use of video between an organi-
      zation and its employees is growing rapidly.   Goes
      into the unique skills and systems needed in corporate
      journalism.   Explains how to communicate with man-
      agement on the cost, content and impact of video
      news on the organization.   Photographs, bibliography,
      and figures.

406   Videolog: Programs for Business and Industry.   New
      York: Esselte Video, Inc., 1979.   275 pp.

      Comprehensive directory published for companies
      and schools using video to train employees and stu-
      dents, to introduce new technologies, and to improve
      interpersonal skills.   Index.

407   Videolog: Programs for the Health Sciences.   New York:
      Esselte Video, Inc., 1979.   400 pp.

A new, totally updated and expanded edition for hospitals, schools, libraries and companies that use video in health care education. Subject index.

21. HOME VIDEO

See also no. 30.

408 Bensinger, Charles. The Video Guide (updated and revised edition). Santa Barbara, Calif.: Video Info
Publications, 1978. 250 pp.

A how-to book on videotape equipment. Describes
the development of video tape technology, limitations
and advantages of popular systems including 1/2-inch
videocassette formats and much more. Photographs,
diagrams, appendixes, glossary, and index.

409 Bunyan, John, and James Crimmins. The Complete
Video Cassette Users Guide. 2nd edition. New
York: Knowledge Industries Publications, 1978.
200 pp.

Completely revised and expanded with sections on
video technology and production; on video use by educational institutions, industry, etc., plus a look at
the future. Illustrations and photographs.

410 Ciccolella, Cathy. A Buyer's Guide to Video Cassette
Recorders. New York: Sterling Publishing Company,
1979. 128 pp.

This handbook discusses the features of all the
principal systems in today's market (Betamax, VHS,
Omnivision and many more) with 31 photographs of
the leading video cassette recorders, video cameras,
and the big-wide-screen projector systems. The author's concise and easy to follow text takes the mys-
tery out of editing, dubbing, film-to-tape transfers
and all the other things you can do with a VCR. Index, appendix, photographs, tables, and figures.

411 Dranov, Paula. Publishing/Programming Opportunities
     in Consumer Video. White Plains, N. Y. : Knowledge
     Industries Publications, n. d.

     Includes the expanding market for productions in
     such fields as cable and pay TV, broadcast syndica-
     tion, domestic satellite distributions, video disc, and
     cassettes. Bibliography, index, and tables.

412 Kybett, Harry. The Complete Handbook of Videocassette
     Recorders. 2nd edition. Blue Ridge Summit, Pa. :
     TAB Books, 1981. 322 pp.

     Contents include introduction to videocassettes,
     simple cassette playbacks, simple recording, opera-
     tional controls and facilities, inter-connection of vari-
     ous types, cueing and editing, copy and special opera-
     tions, limitations, general care and maintenance, and
     more. Index, diagrams, photographs, and illustra-
     tions.

413 Maltin, Leonard, and Allen Greenfield. The Complete
     Guide to Home Video. New York: Harmony Books,
     1981. 182 pp.

     Survey of the home video field, including cassette
     and video disc. Lists feature films available and
     sources, as well as equipment. Good reference.

414 Video Industry Directory. New York: Savvy Manage-
     ment, Inc. , 1981. 250 pp.

     Includes films active in the home video industry
     plus general industry information.

415 The Video Sourcebook. 2nd edition. Syosset, N. Y. :
     The National Video Clearinghouse Inc. , 1980. 1259
     pp.

     Lists video programs for rent and purchase for
     any video player. Over 15, 000 titles listed. Index.

416 Videolog: Programs for General Interest and Entertain-
     ment. New York: Esselte Video, Inc. , 1979. 300
     pp.

     Source for a wealth of information on over 4500
     programs and series for home video owners, schools,
     libraries, businesses, and community groups. Index.

22. VIDEOTEXT

417 Fedida, Sam, and Rex Malik. Viewdata Revolution. London: Associated Business Press, 1979. 168 pp.

As defined by the authors, a new medium that is as critical to the development of the "third" industrial revolution as were the steam engine to the first and the internal combustion engine to the second. Chapters include information retrieval, electronic mail, electronic funds transfer, education, etc. This system is one of many being developed around the world, all utilizing video. Interesting peek at the future of alternative video systems. Index, appendix, tables, figures, and photographs.

418 Rutowski, Katherine, editor. Videotex Services. Washington, D. C.: National Cable Television Association, 1981. 154 pp.

Provides overviews of the competing systems, introducing videotex, regulation, new entrants in the field, the future of cabletex, etc. Glossary.

419 Sigel, Efrem, editor. Videotext: The Coming Revolution in Home/Office Information Retrieval. White Plains, N. Y.: Knowledge Industry Publications, 1980. 154 pp.

This book contains first hand reports on the BBC's Ceefax service to England, on the British Post Office's project and on various tests of these technologies in the U. S. by C. B. S., Knight-Ridder, GTE, and others. It is a state of the art report on this new use of television and computers. Index, appendixes, and photographs.

420 Viewdata and Videotext, 1980-81: A Worldwide Report.

White Plains, N. Y. : Knowledge Industries Publications, 1980. 622 pp.

Transcript of an international meeting. Included are papers on videotext in Canada, the United States, France, the United Kingdom, and Japan. Subjects covered include design and evaluation, market projects, international standards, electronic publishing and private systems. Illustrations.

421 Woolfe, Roger. Videotex: The New Television/Telephone Information Services. Philadelphia: Heyden and Son, Ltd. , 1980. 170 pp.

This book describes the world of videotex systems, which is the result of linking domestic televisions to remote computers using the normal telephone network, and providing a whole new method of information communication. It was written for readers who are not familiar with videotex, but who want to gain a broad overview of what it is all about and where it is going. The book is international in scope. Glossary, figures, photographs, and tables.

23. SATELLITES

422 Belendiuk, Arthur, and Scott Robb. Broadcasting via
Satellite: Legal and Business Considerations. New
York: New York Law School, 1979. 175 pp.

This book provides an overview of the satellite
communications technology now applied to the basic
U. S. broadcasting system. It covers areas such
as technical requirements, application procedures,
the regulatory process and business planning considerations. The book offers a detailed examination
of the operational and organizational changes presently
taking place throughout the broadcast industry through
the introduction of satellite technology. Index, glossary, and illustrations.

423 DeWalt, Gary. The Communications Satellite Handbook.
New York: Praeger Publishers, 1981. 320 pp.

Provides a basic, clear introduction to communication satellite technology. Relates the means by
which data--audio and video--are moved from point
to point by the satellites. Reviews their history,
suggests their future uses, and describes the economic and political/regulatory environment in which this
technology has emerged and will continue to operate.

424 Pelton, Joseph N. , and Marcellus S. Snow, editors.
Economic and Policy Problems and Satellite Communications. New York: Praeger Publishers, 1977.
256 pp.

Discusses key critical issues in satellite communications. Defines the problems, establishes a theoretical background, analyzes proposed solutions and
suggests actions to be taken. Covers effects of tech-
nological change on the industry.

425 Signitzer, Benno. Regulation of Direct Broadcasting
     from Satellites: The UN Involvement. New York:
     Praeger Publishers, 1976. 124 pp.

     Investigates the nature and involvement of UN Outer
     Space Committee's seven-year attempt to regulate the
     development and application of this potentially explo-
     sive technology, which makes it possible for one na-
     tion to beam radio and TV signals directly to homes
     in another country.

426 Smith, Delbert D. Communication via Satellite: A Vi-
     sion in Retrospect. Leyden, Netherlands: A. W.
     Sijthoff, 1976. 335 pp.

     Traces the development of the communication satel-
     lite from its origins in the 1800's to its present ad-
     vanced state. Satellite's progress is studied in an in-
     stitutional, legal, and social context. Acronyms, bib-
     liography, and index.

427 Smith, Delbert. Space Stations: International Law and
     Policy. Boulder, Colo. : Westview Press, 1979.
     264 pp.

     This is a study of the potential impact of space
     stations in terms of international law and policy with
     an emphasis on institutional concerns regarding own-
     ership and operation of those structures. The author
     includes an analysis of applicable international treaties
     and conventions and of their effects on space station
     development plus a review of current international law
     and policy issues in the context of operational space
     stations. Photographs, figures, notes, appendix, and
     index.

428 Snow, Marcellus S. International Commercial Satellite
     Communications: Economic and Political Issues of
     the First Decade of Intelsat. New York: Praeger
     Publishers, 1976. 192 pp.

     Finds that INTELSAT, considered as an interna-
     tional public utility, is basically satisfactory. But
     recommended that such important satellite programs
     as health education should be pursued by organiza-
     tions with separate funding.

24. BIBLIOGRAPHIES

429 An Annotated Bibliography of UNESCO Publications and Documents Dealing with Space Communication, 1953-1977. Paris: UNESCO, 1977. 102 pp.

Consolidated list of papers, reports, articles, and publications produced by UNESCO in the field of space communications.

430 "A Bibliography of Selected Rand Publications (Television and Communications Policy)." Santa Monica, Calif.: The Rand Corporation, 1981. 38 pp.

Topics include both broadcast and cable television.

431 Blum, Eleanor. Basic Books in the Mass Media. 2nd edition. Urbana, Ill.: University of Illinois Press, 1980. 426 pp.

An annotated, selected booklist covering general communications, book publisher, broadcasting, editorial journalism, film, magazines, and advertising. Like the previous edition, the new one covers books published in the United States, Canada, Great Britain, Australia, and other English-speaking countries. An excellent reference.

432 Kittross, John M., comp. A Bibliography of Theses and Dissertations in Broadcasting: 1920-1973. Washington, D. C.: Broadcast Education Association, 1978.

As the name implies, this is a listing of theses and dissertations completed from 1920 to 1973 in the field of broadcasting.

433 McCavitt, William E. Radio and Television: A Selected

Annotated Bibliography. Metuchen, N. J. : Scarecrow
Press, 1978. 229 pp.

Collection of the literature written between the
years 1920 to 1976. Contains 1100 listings. Includes selected books and other printed materials
associated with the field of broadcasting, including
cable television. Contains most of the major works
in the field, with annotations. Index and cross-ref-
erences.

434 Middleton, Karen P. , and Meheroo Jussawalla. The
     Economics of Communication: A Selected Bibliography
     with Abstracts. New York: Pergamon Press, 1981.
     249 pp.

Published in cooperation with the East-West Communication Institute, this 386-item bibliography focuses
on works which deal with the "economic analysis of
communications media and channels. " Four category
divisions--definitions, description, analysis, and im-
pact--are utilized and a summary of each entry is
provided.

25. ANNUALS

A. RADIO

435 Duncan, James Jr. American Radio. Kalamazoo, Mich.:
J. H. Duncan c/o Gilmore Advertising (annual revi-
sion--with supplement), 1978. 300 pp.

Published twice per year. Each edition uses data
from the latest Arbitron and Mediastat sweeps. These
data are consolidated and condensed into concise reports for each rated market. In addition, there are almost 100 pages of tables, graphs, and rankings which
give the reader an excellent overview of the radio industry.

B. TELEVISION

436 "The Video Register." White Plains, N.Y.: Knowledge
Industry Publications, Annual.

Directory listing video users, manufacturers,
dealers, production/post production houses and video
publishers and distributors who have programs for
sale or rent.

C. CABLE TELEVISION

437 Brily, Sharon, and Shirley Kwan. Cable Television State
Regulation. Washington, D. C.: Cable Television
Bureau Federal Communications Commission, Annual.

A survey of franchising and other state laws and
regulations on cable TV.

438 1980 Cable Advertising Directory. Annual. Washington,
     D. C., 1980. 425 pp.

     First comprehensive directory of systems that ac-
     cepts advertising with data on more than 600 systems.

439 CATV and Station Coverage Atlas. Washington, D. C.:
     Television Digest, Inc., Annual.

     Guide to communities and areas in relation to the
     predicted coverage of TV stations plus 35-mile zone
     maps depicting areas within 35 miles and 55 miles
     of TV markets. Both commercial and non-commer-
     cial stations are included. There is also a variety
     of other information.

D. ADVERTISING

440 Advertising Age Yearbook, 1981. Annual. Chicago:
     Crain Books, 1981. 304 pp.

     Most material is from the pages of the weekly
     Advertising Age. Divided into four parts including
     special features, a collection of advertising from dif-
     ferent media, top advertisers of the year, and a ma-
     jor "Year in Review" section. Tables, illustrations,
     and photographs.

E. GENERAL

441 Annual Directory of Religious Broadcasting. Morristown,
     N. J.: National Religious Broadcasters. Annual.

     A geographic list of both radio and television sta-
     tions in the U. S., giving for each entry: address,
     ownership, network, frequency, class, representative,
     and chief personnel.

442 Frost, J. M., editor. World Radio TV Handbook: A
     Complete Directory of International Radio and Tele-
     vision. New York: Billboard Publications, 1966.
     Annual.

     Detailed information by country of radio and TV
     stations and broadcasting organizations in 228 coun-

tries. Shortwave, longwave, and mediumwave stations are listed separately by frequency.

443 Hutchon, Jim. BSO Directory of Broadcasting. Wivenhoe, Colchester, U. K.: BSO Publications Ltd. Annual.

An up-to-date international reference for broadcast equipment and broadcast agencies.

444 Wilholt, G. Cleveland, and Harold deBock, editors. Mass Communication Review Yearbook. Volumes 1 and 2. Beverly Hills, Calif.: Sage Publications, 1980.

Consists of various articles on communication theory, methodology, policy issues, information processing, and news reporting.

26. PERIODICALS

A. RADIO

445 <u>Directory of Radio Programming</u>. Universal City, California: Independent Radio Producers, 1981. Quarterly. 146 pp.

Directory listings with formats, music programs, features, networks, and news services, custom services, and a master vendor list.

446 <u>RadioNews</u>. Washington, D. C. : Phillips Publishing Inc. Bi-weekly.

Newsletter dealing with latest developments in all areas of the radio broadcasting industry.

B. TELEVISION

447 <u>Channels of Communications</u>. New York: Media Commentary Council, Inc. Bi-monthly.

Another magazine dealing with television. According to the editor, <u>Channels</u> will be concerned with issues, ideas, informed commentary and investigative reporting.

448 <u>Re:Act</u>. Newtonville, Mass. : Action for Children's Television Inc. Quarterly.

Action for Children's Television news magazine.

449 <u>Telecommunications Reports</u>. Washington, D. C. Published weekly.

Periodical devoted to telecommunications activity,

particularly valued for the wide range and detailed account of the news carried.

450   Television and Children.   Princeton, N. J. :   National
       Council for Children and Television.   Quarterly.

       Deals with the effects of television on children.

451   TV World.   London: Alain-Charles Publishing Ltd.
       Monthly.

       International business magazine for television.

C.   VIDEO

452   Home Video.   United Business Publications, Inc. (475
       Park Avenue South, New York).   Monthly.

       Another of the new magazines dealing with video
       and home video in particular.   Articles include sub-
       jects such as available programs for home use on
       video tape, reports on new video equipment, and how
       to produce your own home TV show.   Has potential
       for home video buffs if articles are kept as diversi-
       fied as the issues examined.

453   Home Video Report.   White Plains, N. Y. :   Knowledge
       Industry Publications, Inc.   Semi-monthly.

       Source of information on home video cassettes,
       discs, programming, hardware, CATV, pay TV.

454   Playback.   Hollywood, Calif. :   U. S. Video Corporation.
       Monthly.

       Newsletter dealing with various aspects of video
       in the U. S.

455   Reel to Real.   Hollywood, Calif. :   U. S. Video Corpora-
       tion.   Monthly.

       Newsletter dealing with video tape.

456   Videodisc News.   Arlington, Va. :   Videodisc Services,
       Inc.   Monthly.

       Articles and other information relating to videodisc
       technology.

457 Videodisc/Teletext. Westport, Conn.: Microform Review, Inc. Quarterly.

Includes features, equipment reviews, international developments, etc.

458 Videofinder, The International Video Program Guide. Madera Beach, Fla.: Videofinder Publications. Monthly.

International video program guide published to serve institutional and private owners of video cassette and video disc equipment.

459 VideoNews. Washington, D. C.: Phillips Publishing, Inc. Bi-weekly.

Newsletter covering management, marketing and regulations of the video industry.

460 The Video Publisher. White Plains, N. Y.: Knowledge Industry Publications. Bi-monthly.

A newsletter about program production and distribution. Covers areas such as broadcast syndication, cable and pay-TV, cassettes and discs, new programming sources, and video technology.

461 Video Review. Farmingdale, N. Y. Monthly.

Covers all aspects of the world of video from reviews to equipment for the home.

462 VU Marketplace. White Plains, N. Y.: Knowledge Industry Publications, Inc. Bi-weekly newsletter.

Newsletter for users and producers of video hardware, programs, and services.

D.   EDUCATIONAL

463 Current--For People in Public Broadcasting. Washington, D. C.: National Association of Educational Broadcasters. Twice-monthly.

Newspaper for public broadcasters. Replaces the Public Telecommunication Letter.

464 ETV Newsletter. Ridgefield, Conn.: C. S. Tepfer Publishing Company. Bi-weekly.

      Bi-weekly news report of educational and instructional television.

465 Public Broadcasting Report. Washington, D. C.: Television Digest, Inc. Bi-weekly.

      Newsletter of public TV, radio, and related fields.

E. ADVERTISING

466 Advertising Age. Chicago, Ill.: Crain Communications, Inc.

      Trade paper for the advertising industry. Contains articles on radio and television advertising.

F. ENTERTAINMENT

467 Backstage. New York: Backstage Publications, Inc. Weekly.

      A service weekly for the communications and entertainment industry.

G. TECHNICAL

468 Fiber Optics and Communications. Brookline, Mass.: Information Gatekeepers, Inc. Monthly.

      Newsletter covering domestic and international news on fiber optics, communications and related fields.

469 Fiber Topics. West Boylston, Mass.: Voltec Corporation. Quarterly.

      Rather technical newsletter concerning fiber optics.

H. CABLE TELEVISION

470 Cable Marketing. Associated Cable Enterprises, Inc.

(488 Madison Avenue, New York). Monthly.

A marketing/management magazine for cable television executives.

471   Cable Reports. Washington, D. C. : Cable Television
Information Center. Monthly.

Newsletter developed to help local officials make informed decisions about telecommunications policy.

I.   INTERNATIONAL

472   Broadcast Communications. Prairie Village, Kan. : Globecom Publishing Ltd. Monthly.

The international journal of broadcast technology.

J.   VIDEOTEXT

473   Viewtext. Brookline, Mass. : Information Gatekeepers, Inc. Monthly.

Newsletter with complete coverage of the worldwide viewdata/teletext market.

K.   SATELLITES

474   Comsat Magazine. Washington, D. C. : Communication Satellite Corporation. Bi-monthly.

Reviews Comsat doings and related subjects.

475   Satellite News. 7315 Wisconsin Avenue, Suite 1200 N.
Washington, D. C. : Phillips Publishing, Inc. Bi-weekly.

Reports on all the developments of satellite communication. Includes the use of satellites for pay TV and cable.

L.   GENERAL

476   Access. Washington, D. C. : National Citizens Committee for Broadcasting. Bi-weekly.

Newspaper dealing with citizens and the broadcast industry.

477   Business Screen.   New York: Backstage Publications, Inc.   Monthly.

Deals with various aspects of both film and video production.

478   Code News.   New York: The Code Authority, NAB. (New York Code Authority Office, 477 Madison Avenue, Suite 1405, New York).   Monthly.

Monthly magazine published by the National Association of Broadcasters containing information concerning that organization's radio and television code.

479   Communications Daily.   Washington, D. C. :   TV Digest, Inc.   Daily.

Coverage includes broadcasting, common carrier, cable, regulations, electronic publishing, etc.

480   Gordon, Thomas F.   Communication Abstracts.   Beverly Hills, Calif. :   Sage Publications, Inc.   Quarterly.

An international information service designed to give thorough, accurate, up-to-date coverage of the most important communications-related literature.

481   Kline, F. Gerald, editor.   "Communication Research." Beverly Hills, Calif. :   Sage Publications.   Quarterly.

An international journal for scholars and professionals exploring issues in communications.

482   Media Law Reporter.   Washington, D. C. :   Bureau of National Affairs.   Weekly.

Published weekly for media counselors and executives, editors, judges, government agencies, and law and journalism schools.   Current court decisions are brought together, carefully headnoted, and indexed for fast easy reference.

483   On Location.   Hollywood, Calif. :   Quarterly.

Magazine dealing with film and videotape production.

484   Telematics.   Brookline, Mass.:   Information Gatekeepers, Inc.   Bi-monthly.

Keeps abreast of the communication field including computers and updated information out of Washington and around the world.

27. REFERENCES

A. TELEVISION

485 Brooks, Tim, and Earle Marsh. The Complete Directory of Prime Time Network Television Shows: 1946-
Present. New York: Ballantine Books, 1979. 848
pp.

Years of extensive research by two top TV net-
work-professionals have gone into the creation of this
most comprehensive, accurate and easy-to-use resource. It is the first book to trace programming back to the founding of the networks and it
provides all the information on every program that
ever aired on night time network TV between 1946
and 1978. Index, appendixes, charts, and photographs.

486 Brown, Les. The New York Times Encyclopedia of
Television. New York: Times Books, 1977. 492
pp.

Information is arranged in chronological order.
Coverage is thorough, including broadcast history,
FCC regulations, cable TV, pay TV, network and
station groups, syndications, and much more. Illustrations and bibliography.

487 Johnson, Catherine, editor. TV Guide 25-Year Index
(1953-1977). Radnor, Pa.: Triangle Publications,
Inc., 1979. 506 pp.

In addition to being a research aid, a glance
through the volume is an educational look at the history of the medium.

488 McNeil, Alex. Total Television. New York: Penguin
Books, 1980. 1087 pp.

This is a book for people who love television and who are as fascinated by the ebb and flow of fashions in programming as by the shows themselves. More than 3400 series, network and syndicated, prime-time and daytime programs are included. It is probably the most comprehensive guide to the small screen ever published; gives network or syndication affiliation, running dates, description of series, and casts. Index.

489 Meringhoff, Laurene, editor. Children and Advertising: An Annotated Bibliography. New York: Council of Better Business Bureau, 1980. 87 pp.

Includes hundreds of books, articles, research reports, and the like. Index.

490 Miller, Carolyn H. Illustrated TV Dictionary. New York: Harvey House, 1980. 135 pp.

Aimed at grade school or young high school students, and provides non-technical definitions for several hundred terms in commercial broadcasting.

491 Steinberg, Corbett, editor. TV Facts. New York: (National Academy of TV Arts and Science) Facts on File, Inc., 1980. 541 pp.

TV Facts is a wealth of facts, statistics and surveys dealing with past and current problems, viewing habits and attitudes, ratings, advertising, awards and the industry in general. Index.

B. CABLE TELEVISION

492 Cablefile/80. Denver, Colo.: Titsch Publishing, Inc., 1980. 600 pp.

Directory for the cable industry that profiles every cable system in the country, discusses FCC cable regulations, has a hotline directory for equipment manufacturers and a listing of the top 100 advertising agencies.

493 Chin, Felix. Cable Television: A Comprehensive Bibliography. New York: IFI/Plenum, 1978. 285 pp.

The first section lists general reference materials,

periodicals, and indexes to periodicals and legal digests. The second contains citations under seven categories including general information and history, cable regulations, cable technology, cable finance, uses of cable TV, cable and education, and community control and franchises. The last section consists of more than 150 pages of appendixes. Glossary, appendixes, and index.

C. PROGRAMMING

494 David, Nina, editor. TV Season 1977-78. Phoenix, Ariz.: Oryx Press, 1979. 282 pp.

TV Season is a guide to everything that happens on television. Special indexes cover new shows, cancelled shows, new shows that were cancelled and shows captioned for the hearing impaired. Every performer, producer, director, writer, and host is listed in the "Who's Who in TV" section. Good reference.

495 Terrace, Vincent, editor. The Complete Encyclopedia of Television Programs 1947-1979. South Brunswick, N.J.: A. S. Barnes, 1979. 1200 pp.

Complete photographic guide to all network and syndicated TV shows, both prime time and all other times, including "soaps," children's shows, game shows, cartoons, talk shows, etc., as well as prime time adventure shows, spies, westerns, comedies, crime and police shows, and all other categories. Index and photographs.

D. SATELLITES

496 Satellite Directory (1981). Washington, D. C.: Phillips Publishing Company, 1981. 515 pp.

Directory includes programming services, earth stations, hardware and technical services, etc. The 1981 edition is similar in form and content to the 1980 directory except that there are about three to four times more entries in most sections and 50 percent more entries in programming and the earth station listings.

E. GENERAL

497 Armstrong, Ben, and M. Lay Vay Sheldon. Religious Broadcasting Source Book. Morristown, N. J. : National Religious Broadcasters, 1976. 200 pp.

Collection of articles taken from issues of "Religious Broadcasting" magazine, some of which were first speeches, others were analytic reviews of things central to Christian communication with broadcasting, etc. Subjects cover how to get started in Christian broadcasting to the Christian commercial. Bibliography.

498 Avery, K. Robert; Paul E. Burrows; and Clara J. Pincus. Research Index for NAEB Journals (1957-1979). Washington, D. C. : National Association of Educational Broadcasters, 1980.

Listing of each article to appear in NAEB Journal, Educational Broadcast Review and Public Telecommunication Review.

499 Bahr, Alice Harrison. Video in Libraries: A Status Report 1979-1980. 2nd edition. New York: Knowledge Industry Publications, 1980. 118 pp.

Assesses the current level of library involvement with video and attempts to answer the questions most librarians have about this medium. Covers topics such as sources of video programming, copyright, equipment and tape. Index, bibliography, appendixes, and photographs.

500 Citizens' Media Directory. Washington, D. C. : National Citizens' Committee for Broadcasting, 1977. 170 pp.

Categories include both national and local media reform groups, public access centers, alternative news services, community radio stations, and film and video producers and distributors.

501 Diamant, Lincoln, editor. The Broadcast Communications Dictionary. 2nd edition, revised and enlarged. New York: Hastings House Publishers, 1978. 208 pp.

Revised and enlarged to include over 4000 terms

in current use in radio and television programming
and production; equipment and engineering; audio and
video recording; advertising, etc.

502 Ellmore, Terry R. The Illustrated Dictionary of Broad-
     casting CATV/Telecommunications. Blue Ridge Sum-
     mit, Pa.: TAB Books, 1977. 396 pp.

     A good source of modern, easy-to-use definitions
     that explain the terminology used in all fields of tele-
     communications. Contains understandable terms used
     in radio, TV, CATV, audio, advertising, graphics,
     journalism, film, acting, law, lighting, sales, pro-
     gramming, etc. Illustrations.

503 Enos, Richard Leo, and Jeanne L. McClaran, editors.
     A Guide to Doctoral Dissertations in Communication
     Studies and Theater. Ann Arbor, Mich.: University
     Microfilms International, 1978. 132 pp.

     Contains more than 7000 dissertation titles or-
     ganized into twelve major categories. Areas covered
     include Communication Theory and Research, Com-
     munication Education, Mass Communication, and more.

504 Friedman, Leslie, editor. Sex Role Stereotyping in the
     Mass Media: An Annotated Bibliography. New York:
     Garland Publishing, Inc., 1977. 324 pp.

     Sections cover the mass media in general, adver-
     tising, broadcasting, media, film, print media, popu-
     lar culture, media image of minority group women
     and of men, children's media, and the impact of me-
     dia stereotype on occupational choices. Index.

505 Gadney, Alan. How to Enter and Win Video/Audio Con-
     tests. New York: Facts on File Publications, 1981.
     193 pp.

     As the publisher suggests, "Everything you need
     to know to win cash prizes, fellowships, grants, and
     broadcast opportunities." The book provides informa-
     tion on more than 401 major contests. Good refer-
     ence if you're looking for places to enter your pro-
     ductions.

506 Gordon, Thomas F., and Mary Ellen Verna. Effects and

Processes of Mass Communication: A Comprehensive
Bibliography, 1950-1975. Beverly Hills, Calif.: Sage
Publications, Inc., 1978. 234 pp.

Material on the mass communications content and
effect with reference to societal sub groups and the
processes by which media operates are explored. The
volume includes entries on such topics as advertising,
censorship, drugs, sexual behavior, politics, music,
and violence.

507 Haight, Timothy R. Journalism Trends: Aspen Institute
Guide to Print and Electronic Journalism Statistics.
New York: Praeger Publishers, 1981. 256 pp.

The book includes a new analytic introduction, plus
chapters on the growth of journalism; ownership and
control; economics of journalism; employment and
training in journalism; content trends, audience, and
U. S. journalism overseas.

508 Jones, Vane. North American Radio-TV Station Guide.
14th edition. Indianapolis, Ind.: Howard W. Sams
and Company, 1981. 210 pp.

A complete up-to-date listing of television, FM
and AM radio stations in the United States, Canada,
Mexico, Cuba, and the West Indies.

509 Kittross, John M., editor. Administration of American
Telecommunications Policy. Two volumes. New
York: Arno Press, 1980.

This two-volume set provides source material basic
to the study of two major aspects of this field. The
first volume provides three landmark studies on the
licensing of broadcast services. The second volume
deals with the organization of telecommunications regulation in the United States, including the 1934 Study
of Communication by an Interdepartmental Committee
that helped shape the Federal Communications Commission.

510 Lewin, Leonard, editor. Telecommunications: An Interdisciplinary Survey. Dedham, Mass.: Artech House
Books, 1979. 657 pp.

As stated in the book, the main purpose of this

volume is to make generally available the basic material constituting the MS Interdisciplinary Program
in Telecommunications at the University of Colorado.
Coverage includes chapters on the FCC, control and
regulation, speech and privacy, the information society, international communications, computers and
engineering concepts. Although parts of the book are
technical in nature, it is still a good reference. Index, references, appendix, and figures.

511 MacDonald, R. H. Print-Broadcast First Amendment
Parity. Washington, D. C.: National Association
of Broadcasters, 1980. 44 pp.

Selections are listed in sections on books and collections, articles in legal periodicals, articles in
general publications, speeches, and other bibliographies. Unannotated citations.

512 Murray, John. The Media Law Dictionary. Washington,
D. C.: University Press of America, 1978. 139 pp.

The first comprehensive dictionary of terms used
in the study and practice of media law. Useful text
for scholars, editors, TV, radio and print journalists,
as well as students in media law courses. Bibliography and appendixes.

513 Rivers, William L., editor. Aspen Handbook on the
Media--1977-79 Edition. Palo Alto, Calif.: Aspen
Institute Publications and Praeger Publishers, 1977.
320 pp.

This new and updated version and expanded edition
continues the tradition of excellence started in 1971.
It is a unique and invaluable reference--the only concise, inexpensive, and comprehensive reference to
the media available today as of the publication date.
Nearly 700 separate listings and descriptions are included in the handbook's survey of the most current
information sources and research activities in the
communications field. Bibliography.

514 Sterling, Christopher H., editor. Dissertations in Broadcasting. 26 books. New York: Arno Press, 1979.

Collection of 26 books, but each may be purchased

individually. The dissertations included here reflect
the industry they cover. Nearly half the dissertations
deal with some aspect of regulation or control. Seven
dissertations trace development of program types or
deal with programming process, and four of these concentrate on the entertainment aspects of TV and radio.
Five or six studies examine organizational/economic
aspects of the industry, including one study of the
only serious attempt at a fourth commercial TV network and two others dealing with monopoly aspects
of network operation in both radio and television.

APPENDIX: UNANNOTATED WORKS

515 Abshire, David. International Broadcasting: A New Dimension of Western Diplomacy. Beverly Hills, Calif.: Sage, 1976.

516 Antitrust, the Media and the New Technology. New York: Practicing Law Institute, 1981. 560 pp.

517 Bellman, Beryl, and Bennetta Jules-Rosette. A Paradigm for Looking. Norwood, N. J.: ABLEX Publishing Corp., 1977. 217 pp.

518 Berlyn, David. Your Future in Television Careers. New York: Richards Rosen Press, 1978.

519 Borwick, John. Sound Recording Practice: A Handbook Compiled by the Association of Professional Recording Studios. London & New York: Oxford University Press, 1976. 440 pp.

520 Brown, Les. Keeping Your Eye on Television. New York: The Pilgrim Press, 1979. 84 pp.

521 Cable Television Information Center. Social Services and Cable TV. Washington, D. C.: Cable Television Information Center, 1976. 250 pp.

522 CBS Office of Social Research. Communicating with Children Through Television. New York: CBS, 1977.

523 Collins, Robert. A Voice from Afar: The History of Telecommunications in Canada. Scarborough, Ontario: McGraw Hill-Ryerson, 1977. 304 pp.

524 Comptroller General of the United States. Suggestions to Improve Management of Radio Free Europe/Radio Liberty. Washington, D. C.: General Accounting Office, 1976. 71 pp.

142

525 Comstock, George. Television in America. Beverly
    Hills, Calif.: Sage, 1980. 154 pp.

526 Cooper, Robert B., Jr. CATV System Management &
    Operation. Blue Ridge Summit, Pa.: TAB Books,
    n. d.

527 Dance, F. R. Broadcast Training Techniques. New
    York: UNIPUB, 1976.

528 Davison, W. Phillips; James Boylan; and Frederick T.
    C. Yu. Mass Media Systems and Effects. New
    York: Praeger, 1976. 245 pp.

529 Diamond, Edwin. Good News, Bad News. Cambridge,
    Mass.: MIT Press, 1978. 263 pp.

530 Ethnicity and the Media. New York: UNIPUB, 1977.

531 Eysneck, H. J., and D. K. B. Nias. Sex, Violence
    and the Media. New York: St. Martin's Press, 1978.

532 Fang, Irving E. Those Radio Commentators. Ames,
    Iowa: Iowa State University Press, 1977.

533 Fletcher, James E., and Stuart H. Surlin. Mass Com-
    munication Instruction in the Secondary School. Falls
    Church, Va.: Speech Communication Association,
    1978. 151 pp.

534 Frost, J. M., editor. World Radio TV Handbook 1980.
    34th edition. New York: Watson-Guptill Publications
    (Billboard Books), 1980.

535 Goldsen, Rose K. The Show and Tell Machine: How
    Television Works and Works You Over. New York:
    Delta, 1978. 441 pp.

536 Hallman, Eugene S.; J. Hindley; and Don Mills. Broad-
    casting in Canada. Ontario: General Publishing Co.,
    Ltd., 1977. 90 pp.

537 Hamburg, Morton I. All About Cable: Legal and Busi-
    ness Aspects of Cable and Pay Television. New York:
    Law Journal Seminar's Press, 1979.

538 Ito, Masami. Broadcasting in Japan. Boston: Routledge
    & Kegan Paul, 1978.

539 MacAvoy, Paul W. Deregulation of Cable Television.
       Washington, D. C. : American Enterprise Institute
       for Public Policy Research, 1977. 169 pp.

540 McLuhan, Marshall. The Mechanical Bride. Boston,
       Mass. : Beacon Press, n. d.

541 Maloney, Martin, and Paul Max Rubenstein. Writing
       for Media. Englewood Cliffs, N. J. : Prentice-Hall,
       Inc. , 1980. 292 pp.

542 Martin, James. The Wired Society. Englewood Cliffs,
       N. J. : Prentice-Hall, Inc. , 1978. 300 pp.

543 Metzler, Ken. News Gathering. Englewood Cliffs, N. J. :
       Prentice-Hall, Inc. , 1979. 375 pp.

544 Molden, Vaughncille. Telecommunications and Black
       Americans: A Survey of Ownership, Partnership and
       Control. St. Louis, Mo. : Center for Development
       Technology and Program in Technology and Human
       Affairs, Washington University, n. d.

545 Nash, Constance. The Television Writer's Handbook:
       What to Write, How to Write it, Where to Sell it.
       New York: Harper & Row, 1978. 186 pp.

546 Norback, Craig T. , and Peter G. Norback, compilers
       and editors. TV Guide Almanac. New York: Bal-
       lantine Books, 1980.

547 On Cable. Norwalk, Conn. : Omni Communications.
       Monthly.

548 Phelan, John M. Mediaworld: Programming the Public.
       New York: Seabury Press, 1977. 169 pp.

549 Porter, William E. Assault on the Media: The Nixon
       Years. Ann Arbor, Mich. : University of Michigan
       Press, 1976. 320 pp.

550 Quick, John, and Herbert Wolff. Small Studio Video
       Tape Production. New York: Addison-Wesley, 1976.
       234 pp.

551 Redfern, Barrie. Local Radio. New York: Focal Press,
       1979.

552 Rubin, Barry. International News and the American
     Media. Beverly Hills, Calif.: Sage, 1977. 71 pp.

553 Rubin, Bernard. Media, Politics and Democracy. New
     York: Oxford University Press, 1977.

554 Scheuer, Steven H., editor. The Television Annual,
     1978-79. New York: Macmillan, 1979.

555 Seiden, Martin H. CATV Sourcebook. Blue Ridge Sum-
     mit, Pa.: TAB Books, n. d. 150 pp.

556 Series, Serials and Packages. Syosset, N. Y.: Broad-
     cast Information Bureau, n. d. Annual with supple-
     ment.

557 Shimanoff, Susan B. Communication Rules: Theory and
     Research. Beverly Hills, Calif.: Sage, 1980.

558 Shook, Frederick, and Dan Lattimore. The Broadcast
     News Process. Denver, Colo.: Morton Publishing
     Co., 1979. 369 pp.

559 Siegan, Bernard H., editor. Regulation, Economics and
     the Law. Lexington, Mass.: Lexington Books, 1979.

560 Soares, Manuela. The Soap Opera Book. New York:
     Harmony Books, 1978. 182 pp.

561 Taylor, Glenhall. Before Television: The Radio Years.
     Cranbury, N. J.: A. S. Barnes, 1979.

562 Television Newsgathering. Scarsdale, N. Y.: SMPTE,
     1976. 168 pp.

563 The Video Handbook. 3rd edition. New York: United
     Business Publications, 1977. 128 pp.

564 Voight, Melvin, and Gerhard Hanneman. Progress in
     Communication Sciences. Norwood, N. J.: ABLEX
     Publishing Co., 1979. 208 pp.

565 Booker T. Washington Foundation. How Blacks Use
     Television for Entertainment and Information. 2 vol-
     umes. Washington, D. C.: Booker T. Washington's
     Cable Communications Resource Center, n. d. 152
     pp.

566 Winslow, Ken, editor. The Video Programs Index. 4th
      edition. Syosset, N. Y. : The National Video Clearing
      House, Inc. , n. d.

AUTHOR INDEX

(This index also includes magazines, journals, societies, and organizations.)

147

.